THE ULTIMATE GARDENING BOOK

4 Gardening Books in 1– Square Foot Gardening,

Container Gardening,

Urban Homesteading and

Vertical Gardening

JOY LOUIS

GET YOUR
FREE GIFT!

WAIT! – DO YOU LIKE FREE BOOKS?

My **FREE Gift** to You!! As a way to say **Thank You** for downloading my book, I'd like to offer you more **FREE BOOKS!** Each time we release a NEW book, we offer it first to a small number of people as a test - drive. Because of your commitment here in downloading my book, I'd love for you to be a part of this group. You can join easily here ➔ http://gardening-mastery.com/

Table of Contents

Chapter 1

SQUARE FOOT GARDENING

Square foot gardening means dividing the growing areas into small square sections. The aim is to plan and create small but intensively planted gardens. A square foot garden is wonderfully manageable. Square foot gardening is perfect for most first gardeners who tend to plant huge unmanageable vegetable gardens. Halfway through the season they have a mass of untended vegetables competing with large cumbersome weeds. There is little yield and the garden experience ends up being very unpleasant. Lower the size of your dream garden a bit with a gardening system that is easy to build, plant, and water. This system has the added plus of providing lush and high yielding crops.

If you hate weeding and bending over until your back screams "enough!", then square foot gardening is for you. You use organic and clean blends of soil. You will have few weeds that come from the ground. What weeds that land in your SFG are very easily pulled out and tossed away.

You build your garden bed from the ground up. It doesn't matter they type of soil is underneath, you create the perfect soil for the vegetables in your raised bed. It is more efficient, and you are concentrating on actually gardening rather than hoeing and pulling weeds.

No more tilling, backbreaking hoeing or trying to keep the ground aerated. You don't have to use fertilizer if you use the recommended blend of soil. The soil you use should provide all the nutrients your fruits and vegetables need.

Not only does square foot gardening use 80 percent less space than row have gardening, but it produces five times as much food. Proper watering is key to success in square foot gardening. Group plants with similar watering needs in squares next to each other. This reduces the chance of overwater or under watering nearby plants.

You do not need as many seeds or plants. You maximize your yield in a small space. Follow the recommended ratios for SFG and your will find that your harvest is much more than with a traditional garden.

Growing your own fruits and vegetables in a square foot garden is organic gardening. Fruits and vegetables from your own garden are high in nutrients and you know they are fresh. As you have your children help in you the garden; you actually increase the chance that your children will eat more of the fruits and vegetables they watched grow.

Growing your own green products gives you the opportunity to reduce the amount of pesticides you use in plant growing. You will definitely save money at the grocery store, and gardening is a great physical activity.

Square foot gardening is a family project. You can give each one of your children their own square foot garden to plan, plant and manage. They will learn the science of growing fruits and vegetables plus a bit of patience and some reasoning skills.

Plants grown in your own garden promote health. These home-grown vegetables and fruits much richer in nutrients and all the phytochemicals, anti-oxidants, vitamin C, vitamin A and folates are in your home-grown vegetables. Home-grown is healthier than those vegetables trucked in to your local grocery store. When you see the fruits of your labors, your sense of satisfaction is unmeasured, plus they really do taste better coming from your own soil.

The environmental pluses of square foot gardening are many. Plant your garden by fruit trees that provide shade as well as fruits, peels, brown leaves and waste to create compost. Turn unattractive areas into wonderful gorgeous landscapes with an awesome raised flower or vegetable beds. Be creative and grow fruits and vegetables together. Your garden will be great to look at, wonderful to harvest, and perfect to eat.

Square foot gardening is a way to get more out of your gardening space. Growing in raised beds is a wonderful method allowing you're the opportunity to use every square inch of your gardening space. You divide the growing area into small square sections that are typically 12" on every side. The aim is to plan and create a small but densely planted garden.

This type of gardening is an awesome hobby. You build your raised beds, fill your boxes with high quality soil and compost, plant the perfect mix of fruit and vegetable crops and you have your own produce department right in your own yard. Combine your square foot garden with a trellis and let tomatoes, grapes, beans and peas grow vertically.

Build your raised bed with wood, but do not used pressure-treated wood. You can also build a raised bed with bricks, cinder blocks or other stones. Try not to use railroad ties; they have chemicals permeating through their wood layers that will stunt the growth of your plants.

Once you have your raised bed built and you have filled it with great soil and compost, don't step on the soil in the raised bed. Stepping on garden soil will compact it, and this destroys the texture you have built up. If you have built your raised bed no more than four feet across, you have no reason to step into the garden.

Divide your raised beds into one foot squares. Use twine or thin pieces of wood to keep your grid even. The idea is to keep squares separated and sow a new crop in one square. Once you now have your space marked, you don't have to guess where one square ends and another begins. Plus, you have an awesome garden when the plants start to grow!

You can purchase vinyl grids or wooden grid systems at your local garden store if you are unsure how to make them yourself. They are inexpensive and you just need to lay down the exact grids in your boxes, and you have the squares ready to garden. (This is great for those gardeners who just want to garden and not do math calculations).

Sow your seeds or plant your plants in a very unique way. Ignore row spacing, but read the recommended spacing between plans and seeds. Keeping plants in a grid versus rows saves room, and you will find that you fit many more seeds and plants into a raised bed than you thought. Plant one crop in each square.

Now that you have this perfectly organized and awesome grid, and plants are growing, it is easier to week, cultivate, and harvest. When one plant is finished producing, just pull it out, amend the soil and plant another crop. This will give you a garden that stays productive the entire season.

Use the square foot gardening method to plant "themed" crops. Use one square for a salsa garden, another for an Italian garden, and perhaps another for a Mediterranean garden. Try a hamburger garden. This includes cucumbers, peppers, tomatoes and mustard seed. Your neighbors will think you are a master gardener.

Square foot gardening is the perfect way to grow your organic crops. Grid growing is manageable, adaptable, and produces high yields of top-quality organic food. One square foot garden unit should measure 16 sq.ft. and produce an average of 130 plants. Only have 64 sq. ft. of growing space? You can still grow fresh lush vegetables in quantities that will have your neighbors begging for the "fruits of you labors."

Chapter 2

PLANNING YOUR SQUARE FOOT GARDEN

Choose the location of your square foot garden in a spot that gets at least six to eight hours of sun. Further scout out the location and plant your garden in an area where the morning sun hits the garden. Morning sun is much better for growing than afternoon sun and a southeast exposure is optimal. You may want to plant your garden close to the house for ease of watering, weeding, and harvesting. However, because you are actually growing a small garden, it can be placed just about anywhere.

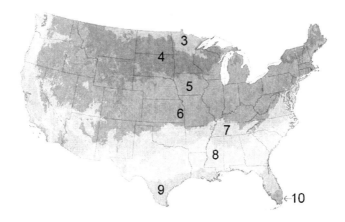

When to start your garden is a varied subject. In the Southeast you can garden for at least three season, but in the north you have a much smaller window of growing time.

Zone Map Key	
3	7
4	8
5	9
6	10

www.burpee.com

This map of the United States give you growing zone information. Plant hardiness zones are based on average lowest winter temperatures. This is a good way to tell when to start planting and how long the growing season lasts.

Zone 3's lowest winter temperatures are -40 to -30°F. Zone 4 is from -30 to -20°F, and if you are in Zone 5 watch for low temperatures of -20 to -10°F. In these zones you may want to start your garden between mid-May and mid-June. Check the hardiness of the plants you want to grow by reading the back of seed packets or the tags on plants starts.

Zone 6's lowest temperatures are from -10 to 0°F, Zone 7 is from 0 - 10°, and Zone 8 is from 10 to 20°F. You can start crops in early to late April in these zones. If you live in Zone 6, however, you may want to start mid-May or after Mother's Day.

If you are lucky enough to live in more temperate climates, Zone 9 is from 20 - 30°F and Zone 10's lowest temperatures range from 30 to 40°F.

The design of your square foot garden is, of course, totally up to you, but usually this type of garden is 4x4 and boxes are placed three feet apart. Some expert square foot gardeners suggest going a little larger with 4x8 square foot boxes and a bit over three feet between the boxes. If you keep these boxes in the 4 ft. range, they will be much easier to water, weed, fertilize and harvest. Try trellising at one end of your square foot boxes. This will double or maybe triple the size of crops you can grow.

Grow your garden where there are not too many trees and shrubs to block sunlight and take up water and nutrients. An open square garden planted in a sunny spot that gets a couple of hours of shade in the hottest part of the day is best.

Chapter 3

BUILDING YOUR GARDEN BEDS

The traditional square foot unit is 4x4 ft., 16 sq. ft. which supplies one person with vegetables and salads for a season. If this square block is a bit unwieldy for you, you can cut your beds down to 3x3 ft. beds. Many gardeners prefer long beds and recommend two parallel beds each 2 ft. wide and 8 ft. long. Include a minimum 15" wide path between and around the beds.

The materials you will need for a traditional square foot garden include:

Square Foot Garden Example (www.instructables.com)

Compost Pile. Composting is Good! (www.nachi.org)

- Four untreated boards, 2"x6"x4'

- Six lath boards that are four feet long

- Ground cloth to prevent weeds

- Wood deck screws

- Soil mixture (you own or purchased)

- Drill

- Dribble for making grids

- Gloves to plants seeds and plants and to get dirty.

Build your boxes by using 2x6 lumber in eight foot lengths. Have your local lumber or big box home store cut your lumber to the proper sizes. Most lumber yards will cut your 2x4s to the lengths you need. Do avoid using treated wood. The chemicals used to treat the wood will leach into the soil in your boxes and ultimately move into the food you eat. Form the boxes and secure the corners with deck screws.

You may be tempted to make larger garden beds than the 4'x4' square. The square foot garden and the 4'x4' bed was designed to keep you from every having to walk and compress the soil within the bed. You can reach every plant in a 4'x4' square.

- Fasten the corners using the deck screws at each corner.

- Roll out the ground cover or weed cloth so it completely covers the area you are going to plant. You may want to overlap the weed cloth to keep the weeds from pushing up through a gap in the fabric.

- Place the wood frame over the weed cloth.

- Fill with compost, soil and plants. Water, harvest and enjoy.

Traditionally planting boxes are usually six to eight inches high, but if you build your boxes with legs you would need to add a bottom panel. Place your boxes on grass and you will need to line it with several layers of newspaper to suppress weeds and grass.

Chapter 4

COMPOST AND SOIL

D ig the ground underneath the boxes down to about six to eight inches. This will give you a soil depth of over a foot. Purchase excellent garden soil in bulk, or have it trucked to your garden space. It does take years to amend local soil for raised beds, so just keep adding soil year after year. Amend your purchased soil by adding compost, sphagnum peat moss and/or composted manure. Be careful, manure may contain weird weeds.

Square foot gardeners do not advise using soil directly from the ground. Most great gardeners use compost and mix it with cleaned bulk soil. Check out the agricultural extension office for sources of good compost suitable for gardening. The local gardening shop or club will also know where you can get the perfect soil for square foot gardening.

You can also make your own compost, which is somewhat time consuming, but fulfilling. You can use kitchen scraps in your compost heap. Using green waste from your kitchen helps the environment by reducing the amount of garbage you produce and send to the land fill.

There are two common types of composting. One is aerobic composting which is the type most gardeners make. You can also do vermicomposting using red wriggler earthworms. Let go of the "yuck" factor; red wriggler earthworms are not a nuisance, they are organic and hygienic.

Make you own compost by layering organic materials like garden clipping, dry leaves, kitchen scraps and shredded paper. Just add a dash of soil to create a concoction that turns into humus. This is the best soil you can use.

- Start a compost pile on bare earth. This allows worms and beneficial organisms to aerate the compost.

- Lay twigs or straw first; just a few inches deep. This is an aid to drainage.

- Add compost materials in layers. Alternate moist and dry materials. Moist ingredients are food scraps, tea bags, coffee grounds; dry materials are straw, leaves and wood ashes.

- Add green ingredients like clover, buckwheat, grass clippings or any other nitrogen sources. This activates the compost.

- Kept the compost pile moist.

- Cover with compost with wood, plastic sheeting, or carpet scraps. Covering will retain moisture and heat.

- You can allow your pile to lie inert form one season to the next if you add enough straw, twigs and brown material.

- Maintain a healthy balance between a balance of carbon and nitrogen-based materials.

- Carbon rich materials like branches and dried leaves give compost a light and fluffy texture.

- Nitrogen is protein rich matter that include food scraps, green lawn clippings and manures.

- Use one-third green and two thirds brown materials in your compost. Brown matter allows oxygen to penetrate and nourish the organisms that reside in the compost. Make sure you do not have too much nitrogen, or you will have a smelly and slowly decomposing anaerobi mess.

If you are a serious gardener, practice hot composting. Gather enough materials to make a pile at least three feet deep. Alternate four to eight inch layers of green materials or kitchen scraps, fresh leaves, coffee grounds plus brown materials like dried leaves, shredded paper and sawdust. Sprinkle water over the pile regularly so it is always the consistency of a damp sponge. Try not to add too much water or the microorganisms in your pile will become waterlogged and drown. If this happens your compost pile will rot.

Compost Pile (www.greenfudge.org)

Check the temperature of the pile with a thermometer on a regular basis. You can also just insert your hand into the middle of the pile to check if it is "warm." If the thermometer reads between 130 and 150°F or feels very warm, your compost is ready to turn.

Turn your compost with a garden fork. Stirring the pile helps it "cook" and prevents material from becoming matted down. When the pile no longer gives off heat and is dry, brown and crumbly, it is cooked and ready to use in the garden.

If you don't have compost you can use leaf-mold, but leaf mold is somewhat short on nutrients. Add a liter of organic fertilizer such as blood meal or ground peanut cake to leaf mold. Fish emulsion is good, but check the label to make sure there are no chemical fertilizers added. Professional gardeners claim that a great trick is to use liquid seaweed emulsion in a watering can every two weeks.

Most square foot gardeners suggest you fill gardening boxes with 1/3 compost, 1/3 peat moss and 1/3 coarse grade vermiculite. Look for organic varieties that contain no fertilizer or chemicals. You can use your own compost or just go buy high grade potting soil.

Chapter 5

WATERING TECHNIQUES

The soil type used in square foot gardening is designed to retain water. This reduces the amount of water used by up to 90 percent compared to traditional row gardening. You do need to keep seeds and transplants moist while germinating and rooting, but the amount of water you use should be reduced once these seeds sprout and the roots take hold. Root crops like carrots and potatoes need to be watered frequently to keep the soil moist. Deep rooted crops like tomatoes and squash prefer deep watering only once per week. Put your root crops in squares next to each other and plant crops with deep roots in another square. Plant crops with medium watering needs in squares between root crops and deep root crops.

Irrigation - Watering Your Garden (www.mysqurefootgarden.net)

Water near the base to prevent water from splashing on to the leaves. Drying water on leaves may promote fungus and diseases.

Water the plants on a regular basis, but don't drown your plants. Square foot gardens are very small and it is best to water by hand. Use water that is room temperature, slightly warmer and water that is warmed by the sun. This helps warm the soil and promote growth. Use warmer water; not hot, in the early stages of the plants' growth.

If you live in an arid or hot climate use a simple irrigation system in the early stages of plant development. You can create your own watering system by taking six to eight water bottles and poking a small hole in each. Use a sewing needle; make very small holes. Fill the bottles with water and use a dribble or your finger to dig a small trench about the length of the bottle in each grid square. Plant the bottle, pin hole down in the soil. The water will slowly drain from the bottles into the soil. You now have a well-watered garden that does not drown your seeds and plants, but releases the water in a small stream. Fill the water bottles back up each morning and do it all over again.

Chapter 6

PLANNING THE PLANTING

Once you have built your 4x4 or 4x8 boxes or 3x3 boxes and filled them with good soil, use a dribble to mark the lines in the soil. You can also use string or purchased grids. Subdivide the boxes according to what you are planting.

Plan your garden to get the most out of you experience. Place tall plants on the north side of your square foot garden. This will keep them from shading the other plants in the garden.

You may want to consider companion planting. This is a process of placing plants that thrive together, near each other. On the same hand do avoid placing plants near each other that will stunt each other's growth.

Now for the spacing part of your square foot garden. SF gardening, according to experts, uses a formula to determine how many plants will fit into each square.

Miniature broccoli and cabbage in each square. Lettuce grown around each plant. (abundantminigardens.com)

- Tomatoes, cabbage, cauliflower, broccoli, eggplant and pepper – 1 plant per square.

- Radish, onions, beets, and carrots – 16 seeds per square.

- Bush beans – 9 seeds per square.

- Pole beans and peas – 8 seeds per square.

- Spinach – 9 seeds per square.

- Lettuce ad parsley – 4 seeds per square.

- Cucumbers – 2 plants per square.

Doesn't sound like too many seeds and plants, but you don't need many. Remember the seeds and plants will grow and begin to take over the squares.

Timing is very important when planting. There are plants that grow well in early spring and some that are late season crops. There are plants that need the heat of the summer and some that grow in a very short time frame. You may have some crops that take the entire growing season to mature. If you plan your square foot garden with the right timing, you can get several crops out of each space before the growing season is over.

For large plants like cabbage, peppers and broccoli, place one plant per square. Make sure you plant it in the center of the square to give it plenty of room.

Large plants like leaf lettuce, Swiss chart and marigolds can be placed 6" apart or four plants per 1" square. Draw a cross in the dirt in your one foot square and divide it into four sections. Than plant one of each vegetable in the center of the smaller squares.

Medium plants like spinach and beets should be planted 4" apart. You can plant up to nine medium plants per square.

Small plants like carrots, radishes and onions can be planted at least 3" apart. This will leave you with 12 plants per square.

Planting seeds is a bit different. For each grid you are ready to plant poke a hole in the dirt with your finger and sprinkle a couple of seeds in the hole. Fill lightly with soil but leave a slight indentation over the area where the seeds are planted. This is to allow water to get to the seeds and the plant's roots once the seeds have germinated.

Carrots grow wonderfully in a square foot garden (freshpet.com)

When the seeds begin to sprout, a good idea is to take scissors and cut off the weaker looking sprouts. This should leave only one sprout per planted area. Note: do not pull the sprouts out. Pulling out the sprouts you don't want will damage the survivor's roots. This causes a weak plant that is susceptible to plant diseases and insects.

Chapter 7

PESTICIDES

Nasturtiums (www.motehrearthliving.com)

To eliminate or reduce the need for pesticides, plants squares of pest deterring plants such as nasturtiums to keep aphids away from tender plants.

Basil complements tomatoes and if planted near tomatoes basil repels mosquitos, aphids, flies and tomato hornworms. Basil might invade your tomato plants, but calm basil down by snipping of flowers before they go to seed. Prune your basil to stimulate the plant to grow bushier. Be careful you don't plant your basil so close to the tomatoes that they are shaded.

Figure 2Carrots from your square foot garden (www.care2.com)

Borage (www.dharanihealingarts.com

Borage or starflower is an annual herb. It tends to repel tomato hornworms and cabbage worms. Borage attract bees for better pollination of other plants. Do watch out, however, borage can be somewhat invasive if allowed to go to seed. They grow to be about 3 feet tall and are scratchy. The stems grow very thick and may require a saw to remove. Plant if you are brave.

Chives deter carrot rust flies and Japanese beetles. They also have awesome purple flowers. Don't let chives go to seed and use them every chance you have for a mild onion-y flavor.

You will probably plant garlic, so plant it by carrots to repel flies. Garlic also keeps rabbits, squirrels and other little critters like snails and mosquitoes way from your plants. Do not plant garlic near beans; garlic will stunt your bean's growth.

Lavender is one of the most beautiful and versatile plants. They attract beneficial insects to the garden and repel fleas and moths. They may spread a bit, but lavender is not invasive. You can use lavender in cooking and recipes and they add a glorious touch to a rose garden.

Chapter 8

Spacing Your Vegetable Plants for Optimal Harvest

There are vegetables that require more space than a square foot garden, but this doesn't exclude them from your garden plans. Planting these larger plants around your square foot garden can stimulate the growth of other plants. It also helps your garden look awesome.

Some plants that require a square of their own are broccoli, cabbage, cauliflowers, okra, tomatoes, peppers and eggplants. In the following illustration, these crops are labeled as "D and A."

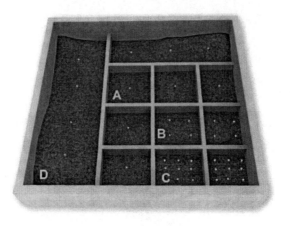

Vegetables that do very well planted four per square are loose leaf lettuces like butter head and romaine (square B). Plant Swiss chard, parsley, leeks, and turnips four in a square.

Plants that do well when planted in a square foot garden are those that enjoy being crowded into 1 foot squares. They produce fast and you can enjoy continual harvests. These crowd-loving plants include radishes, carrots, beets, green onions, and celery.

Add vegetables that love to grow on a trellis to the perimeter of your garden. Be careful not to plant the plants where they will shade the main garden. You can plant snap peas on a trellis, and corn in a short row at the perimeter. Summer squash or zucchini fit in nicely on the edges of your garden. Work in large plants into your square foot garden like peas or melons, cucumbers and pole beans. Trellis tomatoes for an excellent crop all season long.

Chapter 9

SECRETS FOR A GREAT VEGETABLE HARVEST

Can you image how awesome it would be to harvest beautiful and organically grown vegetables from a square foot garden? It just take a little ingenuity and a bit of work, but you can make the most of your garden space with seven little secrets.

Staggered Plantings (www.rodalesorganiclife.com)

- Use the right soil. Organically rich soil is the key to healthy, extensive roots on vegetables that reach deep down for more nutrients and water. Make your square foot beds areas that yield up to four times more than the same number of plants set out in rows. Use loose, fertile soil, efficient spacing, and organic fertilizers.

- Some gardeners feel that the shape of beds does make a difference. Raised beds are more space-efficient if you gently round the tops and form an arc. Rounding the tops increases your total planting area and you have a 20% gain in planting space.

Space your plants smartly to get maximum yields from each square foot bed. Arrange your plants and avoid planting in rows.

Stagger the plants. Don't space your plants too tight. If plants are crowded they might not reach their full yield.

- Grow up. Using a square foot garden combined with a vertical garden will increase the amount of vegetables you get from a harvest. Vertical gardening is perfect for space hungry vining crops like tomatoes, pole beans, peas and squash and cukes.

- Mix up your square foot gardening beds. Plant compatible plants next together and add flowers among the vegetables.

Square Foot Garden (www.jysquarefootgarden.net)

Succession planting is very doable in a square foot garden. You can harvest three or four crops from a single area if you are persistent. An early crop of leaf lettuce can be followed by a bed of squash. Use transplants, choose varieties that are fast growing, and replenish the soil with ¼ to ½ inches of compost every time you replant. Work new compost into the top few inches of you existing soil.

- Square foot gardening is the perfect way to stretch your growing season. Add a few weeks to the end of the growing season by keeping the air around your plants warm. Use mulches, cloches, or even cold frames. You can grow lettuce, kale and turnips or even more tomatoes at the end of the season if you keep them warm.

- One trick to get plants growing faster: heat it up. Use two blankets, one that warms the air and one that warms the soil in early spring. About six weeks before the last frost, preheat cold soils by covering it with black plastic. Next, cover the bed with a slitted clear plastic tunnel. Watch for the soil temperature to reach about 65°F, set out your plants and cover the black plastic with straw. When all danger of frost has passed, remove the clear plastic tunnel and the straw.

Square foot vegetables! (www.yelp.com

Newly harvested vegetables (www.gttymags.in))

Chapter 10

HARVESTING YOUR SQUARE FOOT GARDEN

Now it is time to enjoy the fruits of your labor. If you planted four squares of green beans, you will harvest about four pounds of beans. Keep harvesting them even though it is the end of the season, and don't let beans get big and bulging. Note: this is what you should be doing all season, picking green beans before they are fat and dry.

If you grew cucumbers in your garden, you will get enough to do some batches of pickles. Harvest your onions and set them out to dry. Onions might just store all winter if you hang them up. One square foot gardener in the neighborhood harvested six pounds of red onions, three pounds of sweet onions and over seven pounds of yellow onions. No more purchasing onions at the local grocery store!

Plant four squares of carrots and by fall most of them will be ready to eat. You might find that your carrots are really funny with forked ends, split open, or doubled. Not matter what your carrots look like, they will still taste awesome and be highly nutritious.

By harvest time, you should have tomatoes, peppers, and square growing out of the squares in your garden. Enjoy the bounty you have produced!

Chapter 11

WINTER MONTHS

You can grow vegetables in square foot or raised beds in the winter. If you have very cold winters you will want to keep beds a bit on the short side (but off the ground), and place some padding around your raised beds. This insulation can be shredded leaves or mulch from your garden or the local nursery.

Some square foot gardeners sink their cold frames into the soil to give more protection from winter weather. You do need to have well-drained soil for cold frames to work in the winter.

Raised sqwure foot bed on a sunny slope
(abundantminigardens.com)

Grow your winter crops in moist soil that is rich in organic matter. Summer crops are a bit more easy-going in mediocre soil, but winter crops need optimum soil to thrive. Add compost, peat moss, well-rotted manure, or other organic matter to your soil. Note: Avoid using raw manure! It will burn you winter plants.

Combine about two inches of organic materials into the top six inches of the soil in your winter square foot garden. Avoid too much nitrogen to your root crops.

The best place for your winter beds is a gentle south slope. Snow melts faster on the south side, and soil that tilts toward the winter sun absorbs a great deal of solar energy and stays warmer. If you don't have a south slope, raise your beds by digging a level base.

When you design your square foot winter vegetable garden, take care to maintain the garden. How much maintenance depends on the climate and if cold frames need regular ventilating on sunny days. Do put your square foot winter garden close to your house in case you have to tromp through deep snow.

Chapter 12

Benefits of a Square Foot Garden

Vegetables from a square foot garden (the-

homeharvetcompany.co.za)

Learn to grow over $700 worth of food in a 100 square foot raised bed. Keep your garden simple and don't include fancy vegetable varieties until you are more expert at gardening. Select vegetables that are expensive at the supermarket and varieties that produce high yields. Consider nutritional value and taste. Home grown tomatoes, broccoli, Brussels sprouts, spinach, and kale are wonderful if you grow them in a square foot garden rather than purchasing them in a square foot grocery store bin.

The typical 100 square foot plot will take about eight hours to prepare. Preparing your square foot garden involves digging, amending, raking, building the boxes, setting up the grids, and planting. Add a drip irrigation system, and mulch and you have an awesome vegetable garden.

If you are longing to be a "green" gardener, begin gardening in a square foot garden. It takes 80% less space than a traditional row garden. Your square foot garden will also use about 75% less water and require almost 90% less work. You don't need to spend hours weeding your garden since you are growing plants in awesome soil, and crowding out the weeds with valuable plants.

Grow in groups rather than rows that makes taking care of your garden easy and efficient. A 4x4 box usually has 16 squares in it. Each square is 12"x12". You plant 16 carrots, nine beans, four spinach plants or five heads of lettuce in these squares. Your square foot garden can hold over 100 spring vegetables and plants. Seeds are not wasted since you are planting efficiently.

Pease from your very own garden (www.\pinterest.com)

Place your square foot garden and open up many avenues in your garden spot. You will enjoy and harvest the best garden you have ever grown. Just find a nice sunny spot that invites the sun for six to eight hours a day. Lay your garden squares or four-sided boxes and separate them by aisles that give you plenty of walking space.

Square foot gardening makes the most of little space for those who have limited land to grow vegetables. You can grow vegetables on patios and decks using a square foot garden/raised bed concept. It is difficult to think of anything negative about a square foot garden and the harvest you get all season long.

Chapter 13

CONTAINER GARDENING

Small scale gardens mean frequent upkeep. You will need to water the plants more often since there is a limited amount of soil in the container. Remember to fertilize the plants in container gardens more often than plants in a bare earth garden. If you don't have any containers, you might have to invest more than you would like in purchasing artsy containers. (Or look around your home and start a container garden in a large bowl, teapot, milk jug, or anything else). All these disadvantages are really nothing. Container gardening brings balance to your life, soul and your garden.

Container gardening dates back thousands of years. The Roman were famous for their gardens, and in Egyptian and Oriental homes plants of every size and color were used to provide ambiance. The Hanging Gardens of Babylon, were one of the Seven Wonders of the World, and their legendary beauty was said to be mind-boggling.

There are thousands of chronicles discussing ancient Indian container gardening using medicinal and edible plants. Religious ceremonies often used container gardening as a way to show respect. In Athens, women placed earthen pots planted with fennel and lettuce as well as wheat and barley around the statue of Adonis. They believed it would bring them a lover. Container gardening brings the magic of planting, harvesting, and enjoyment to a variety of situations. If you are a flower garden lover, container gardening is the perfect way to "worship" gardening.

Overflowing pots, tubs, barrels and funky containers add appeal to a garden. Container gardens are practical. It is ideal for those with little to no gardening space or those who want to add architectural interest to an already growing flower or vegetable bed. Container gardens are perfect for growing a variety of vegetable crops. You can do a unique herb garden with basil, chives, thyme and other herbs and sit that container in a sunny spot right outside the kitchen door.

Container gardening adds versatility to gardens that are large or those that are small. They provide instant color and a focal point in the garden. You can use containers to tie the house to the garden. Place containers on the ground or a pedestal. Mount them on a windowsill or hang them from the porch. Matching containers on either side of your front walkway serves as a welcome sign, and containers on a patio add color and ambiance to an outside sitting area.

Clusters of pots can contain a collection of flowers and plants. You can plant just about any plant in a container. How about your houseplants? In decorative pots, they summer outdoors in the garden and make a great addition to your outside space. Add a window box or a hanging basket to your home, and you have instant appeal.

Container gardens are great for beginning gardeners. It is a relative inexpensive hobby, and you can watch your creations grow. Container gardening provides an opportunity to save seeds and trade with other gardeners or just create future plants for yourself. Great advantages of container gardens; less back pain and you can just adjust the height of the pots to your preference.

You can move your garden around to different areas if you grow things in a container. You might need to bring your plants indoors during cool months, which makes an awesome addition to inside environments. There are so many varieties of containers available that you can design a very artistic garden. A couple of huge advantages to container gardening for many gardeners? You won't have pets trampling through your container garden, and weeds tend to stay on the ground rather than in the container. You can see insects, replant when you want, change the theme of the container garden, and so many more advantages.

Chapter 14

CHOOSING THE CONTAINERS FOR YOUR GARDEN

Think outside the norm - container gardening at
its most gorgeous (www.southernliving.com)

It is so fun to pick out the containers for your garden. Think outside your normal ceramic or terracotta pot. One enthusiastic neighbor down the street uses a row boat each year for her plantings. Pumpkins, marigolds, tomatoes and other unrecognizable flower plants grow in this boat. It is very eclectic, and she gets her picture in the gardening news of the local newspaper every year. Another friend plants pumpkins in large broken pieces of pottery. She trains the plants to grow up and over an unsightly fence. Not only does this create a fantastic look to her fence, but she has pumpkins for Halloween decorations.

Some tips and tricks to remember about container gardens, light colored containers are less likely to absorb heat. They will keep roots cool during warm months. Put heavy or oversized pots and containers on a platform with wheels. Wheels will make it easier to move the container when you need to and where you want.

When planting in containers remember that you need to match the size of the plant to the container. A small pot will hinder the growth of full sized tomato or lavender plant. Tomatoes need stakes and room to grow to their full potential. Make sure the container anchors the weight of the plant when heavy laden with warm, ripe fruits. Anchoring your vegetable and large flower plans will keep the plants from breaking the stems and rotting on the ground.

You may not want to plant garlic in an oversized pot. Garlic will grow much better in a shallow container. A friend with a small condo space planted peas in one container, cucumbers in another, garlic and tomatoes in another. She placed the pots against the deck rails and trellised them. The effect was very adorable.

Experiment placing different plants near each other when creating your container garden. Mix and match plants of different types and sizes. Try a tall plant in a large container or a vine that tumbles over the side of a lower container. You can plant vegetable and flowers together in a pot or use different styles and colors of pots grouped together to compliment your flowers and vegetables. A very nice arrangement down the street was a grouping of cherry tomatoes, chili peppers, and purple petunias. Pink begonias and leafy coleus set off the very unusual arrangement.

Make your containers by finding things that can hold dirt. Anything can be a container. A new meaning for the "pot" is a toilet cistern in a greenhouse garden. How about your old tea kettle. You can reuse it as a watering can or recycle into a planter. Plant in an old urn or an old fashioned water pitcher to use as a centerpiece on an outside table. Colanders are perfect used as a container. Plant vegetables, flowers or herbs in a colander; you have instant holes for drainage.

Before using any old thing for a container, check the material of the skin. Is it safe and the surface porous? Terracotta pots are fun, but extremely porous and absorb and leach water and fertilizers through the surface.

Stay away from pots contaminated with lead or asbestos. Lead is a naturally occurring metal, but it is poison to all forms of life. Avoid old containers coated with lead paint or building materials that may have asbestos remnants.

If you want to renovate an interesting piece of furniture from a salvage shop, find out the age of the materials first. Don't use painted materials for a garden planter if you can't determine if they are safe. Use them as a decoration without a plant, but maybe as a complementing accessory

If you have something that you love, and want to use it as a container for your garden, just get creative. Use a liner or as a cachepot or a decorative container used to conceal a smaller pot. One pot inside a larger pot is called double potting, and helps keep your plants safe.

Find the lettuce! Unique boxes and buckets filled
with edibles (www.southernliving.com)

Whatever you do to your container garden let it reflect your
personality. Add collectibles to your containers, use an old chest of
drawers and plant in the drawers, use inexpensive figurines to set
off your plants in the container. The sky is the limit!

Chapter 15

CONTAINER GARDEN ESSENTIALS

Container gardens are highly versatile and manageable. You can grow ornamental and edibles in containers of just about any shape or size. You do need to follow several essential tips and tricks to keep your container garden growing and looking beautiful. It is easy to care for a container garden, just remember they require extra watering and feeding, lots of sunlight, and pruning.

Watering, Pests and Fertilizer

Water your container gardens frequently. Potting soil dries out much quicker than regular garden soil and in really hot weather you may have to water more than once a day. If you let your vegetables go dry just one time, you may stunt the growth of your vegetables and spoil the harvest.

Stick your finger in the soil. This is the easiest way to determine if your container garden needs water. If the top few inches of soil are dry, you need to water. Tip the container on its side. If the soil is dry the container will be lighter.

Vegetable container garden and watering system (www.urganorganicgardener.com)

Water thoroughly. Wetting dry potting soil is a bit different than watering a regular garden. The root ball of the plants may shrink a bit and pull away from the side of the pot as the soil dries. You may find that the water slushes down the side of the container and doesn't wet the soil. To prevent this problem fill the top of the pot with water more than once so the root ball can absorb the water and begin to expand. Do avoid overwatering, however. (You can tell if you have overwatered if the water starts to flood over the sides of the container and run quickly though the drainage holes in the bottom. Stop watering at that point.)

Good water drainage is vital for container gardens. If you are using a container that does not have a hole in the bottom, put coarse materials in the bottom of the container. This will keep the plants' roots out of excess water.

Note that putting gravel in the bottom of a pot with holes does nothing to ensure good drainage. Water naturally flows toward inner material not away from it. Large air spaces between pieces of gravel will not help with drainage. Gravel or clay shards just prevent soil from exiting though the holes.

Fertilize frequently. Nutrients are leached from the soil when you frequently water container gardens. Fertilize your plants at least every two weeks. You can use a liquid or water-soluble fertilizer to get your plants the best nutrients right down to the roots. Find organic fertilizers if you can.

Watch out for pests. Container grown plants have fewer pest problems since they are generally isolated from other plants. Sterilized potting soil does not have disease spores and insects are not lying in wait just to jump on your plants. However, if you do find pests, get rid of them quickly so your whole container is not wiped out.

Chapter 16

THE RIGHT SOIL IS CRUCIAL

When developing a container garden all you need to do is fill pots with soil, stick in the plants and add more soil. Give it some water and viola! you have a container garden. It's almost that easy. Tricks that will help your container garden stay gorgeous, grow healthy vegetables and awesome flowers, plus save you money are:

- Avoid filling your container with soil straight from the garden. Even if your garden is so very wonderful and has the very best soil that money can buy, garden soil is too heavy for containers. It is also too full of weed seeds, bugs and eggs, bacteria and other gunk, plus it will not drain properly. Use potting soil or potting mix or container mix. Potting soil is aerated, sterile, and lightweight in addition it is made from organic materials and mineral particles. Potting soil is really soilless; it doesn't really contain any dirt.

- You can get potting soil in bulk if you need. Tryout different brands to discover which ones you like the best. Don't' worry about choosing the wrong potting soil. Plants will love it no matter what brand you purchase.

- Be aware that you will need a great deal of potting soil, but you don't need to fill the pot to the top. Most vegetable roots only go 10 to 12 inches into the soil. If you add more than that you are wasting potting soil. A good trick is to put plastic soda and milk bottles in the bottom of your container. Throw in the soil. The container will be light and easy to move and you are recycling. You have "killed two birds with one stone", plus you are saving money and being "green."

- Don't use the same soil year after year. Planting in the same soil from last year will not be good for your plants. Soil nutrition gets depleted and the soil probably has undiscovered diseases, fungal spores and insects. Just throw the old potting soil in your regular ground garden. Clean out your pots, wash out with water, and refill with this year's soil.

Self-watering containers (kriscarr.com)

If you are truly an environmentalist, make your own potting soil. Combine a bit of dirt, some aged compost and a handful of sand. By making your own potting soil you have complete control over your plants. This will be a great, inexpensive medium for your garden seedlings, container gardens or house plants. Making your own potting soil gives you the opportunity to choose your own nutrients and you can avoid using commercial chemicals. A good potting soil is easy to handle, drains well, and contains a great deal of organic matter.

Chapter 17

HOMEMADE
POTTING SOIL RECIPE

Use the right soil and this is what you get! (www.

botanical-journeys-plant-guides.com)

For homemade potting soil, add a little bit of garden soil to add density plus is already available. However, do not use garden soil containing pesticides, chemical fertilizer residues or environmental pollutants. Solarize your common garden soil by covering a pile of garden soil with clear, plastic sheeting for four to six weeks. Covering your garden soil with plastic will kill weed seeds, pests and pathogens. You can also sterilize your garden soil in your oven or microwave, but this methods takes a long time and is, well, dirty.

You next need compost. Compost contains beneficial microbes and has a great water-holding capacity and nutrient content. If you make compost yourself, you have a free supply. Make sure it is fully decomposed and screened into a small and consistent size.

Add sand to your mix. Coarse builder's sand improve drainage, add weight to the mix and provides physical support for roots and growing plants.

You will need sphagnum peat moss. Peat moss is a stable ingredient that take s a long time to break down. It is very inexpensive and bulks up mixes without adding weight. It holds water well.

Composed pine bark lightens up soil mixes. It increases pore sizes and allows air and water to travel freely. It is very slow to break down, but beware, pine bark can rob nitrogen from the soil.

Perlite or volcanic rock is heated to become a lightweight and sterile addition to potting soil. It holds three to four times its weight in water and increases pore spaces. Drainage is improved with perlite. You can use perlite in place of sand if you prefer.

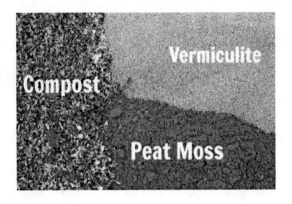

Making your own soil for container gardening onehundreddollarsamonth.com

Add vermiculite to your mix. Vermiculite is a mined mineral that is conditioned by heating. It expands into light particles is used to increase the porosity of soil mixtures. Vermiculite adds calcium and magnesium to the soil. Be careful when handling vermiculite, it does contain asbestos.

Limestone is necessary to adjust the pH of soil mixes that have sphagnum peat or composited pine bark.

You will also need additional nutrient sources if your soil mixture does not contain compost. Natural fertilizers that come from mined minerals, animal byproduct or manures are perfect. A combination of natural fertilizer provides a stable and eco-friendly source of nutrients. Your organic fertilizer blend should contain combinations of alfalfa meal, blood meal, bone meal, cottonseed mean and crab meal. Look for fertilizers with fish meal, greensand, kelp meal and dehydrated manures plus rock phosphate.

If you are mixing large quantities of potting soil, you can use a cement mixer or compost tumbler. Mix very thoroughly so you product is consistent.

General Potting Soil Mix
6 Gallons of sphagnum peat moss
¼ cup limestone
41/4 gallons vermiculite or perlite
41/4 gallons of compost.
Mix together 2 cups of rock phosphate, 2 cups of greensand, and ½ cup of bone mean. Mix in 4 ¼ gallons of compost. Mix 2 cups of rock phosphate, 2 cups of greensand, and ½ cup of bone meal. Add ¼ cup kelp meal, mix, and add 1 ½ cups to your general potting mix.

Use your newly developed potting soil quickly. Avoid storing it to prevent the nutrients from floating away.

Chapter 18

PLANTING A CONTAINER GARDEN

A colander container, and some funky decorations (homehardware.ca)

Plant Strawberries in a container and keep it indoors or out. (dougoster.com)

A container garden is a living flower or vegetable arrangement. Keep your container garden looking and growing great by making sure the roots are healthy and the foliage gets enough sunlight. One type of plant in a container is the simplest to maintain, but plants that thrive in like soil with the same watering and light conditions can make successful combinations.

The plants that are most suitable for container gardening are the ones that can grow in small spaces. Dwarf or those plants that bear fruit over a longer period of time are also good. Read the information on the vegetables you want to plant. Most tomatoes, peppers, cucumbers, squash and eggplants require full sun and containers can be placed in sunny areas. You can grow leafy vegetable like lettuce, cabbage, collards, mustard greens, spinach and parsley in more shady areas. Root vegetables like turnips, beets, radishes, carrots and onions will grow in shady conditions, and most herbs will perform well in full sun or partial shade locations.

Choose a theme when planting a container garden. This will give your container garden an organized look and feel. Consider complementary colors and the back ground where you will leave your container. Just choose your favorite colors and mix and match. Any combination will look awesome. Follow the color wheel or just use your imagination. Mother Nature isn't picky about the colors she puts together, so why should you be?

You do need to think about the lighting, don't put shade loving plants together with sun worshipers. This would be a disaster. Pick plants that have similar requirements. For example, plants that thrive in dry climates have thick and waxy leaves to hold moisture. Their roots like to dry out between waterings. Add them together in one container. Grow different succulents together, and they will provide an awesome artistic garden for you.

Chapter 19

VEGETABLES IN A CONTAINER

You can grow vegetable in contains from large pots to five gallon buckets or half barrels. Plant a single tomato plant or several small vegetables like broccoli or cabbage. Pick out dwarf or bush forms of tomatoes, pumpkins, and winter squash. They are most suited to container gardening. Avoid the pumpkins or tomatoes or winter squash that will grow to huge sizes, they might break your containers.

Salad garden in a container (greenerlifes.com)

Plant a salad container garden. Use different lettuces, cherry tomatoes, parsley or chives. Add a cucumber plant for interest. Plant a pizza garden with basil, tomatoes and peppers. You can also plant container that have edible flowers like pansies, nasturtiums and marigolds.

Plants that only grow for one season are annual plants and these container gardens only last for one season. Annual plants are awesome in containers. Look for those plants that love the warm weather and bloom all summer. Geraniums, marigolds, begonias, scarlet sage and nicotiana are wonderful choices. There are many more annual plants that are awesome in container gardens. Experiment. The beauty of a container garden; if one plant doesn't work, pull it out and plant another type.

Perennial container gardens are those planted with hardy perennials and shrubs that will grow from year to year and season to season. Hostas and daylilies are good perennial container plants. You can also try European wild ginger, ferns, sedges, lavender and sedums. Ornamental grass works well in containers as do dwarf conifers.

Chapter 20

SEEDS IN A CONTAINER GARDEN

You can plant any type of seed in a container garden. You just need to read the package to determine the water, sunlight and soil needs. However if you are using a container garden to grow seedlings for transplanting in your outside ground garden, there are different techniques.

Containers should be at least three inches deep with small drainage hole. You can use plastic containers or plastic plant pots or even half-gallon milk cartons cut lengthwise. Purchase a good quality seed starting mix that is available from a good nursery or garden center. Add water to the seed starting mix and combine. Your soil needs to be thoroughly moistened before you fill the containers. Fill the container to an inch below the top and tap it to settle the mix. Make a seed furrow about ¼ inch deep and drop in an individual seed. Make sure the seeds are an inch a part. Sprinkle starting mix to fill the furrows and pat firmly but gently. Use a spray bottle to water the seeds.

Love lettuce? Plant in a container! (www.ellenogden.com)

As your seedlings sprout, watch them and move them to a warm and sunny spot. Keep the containers moist and watered. When your seeds have given you seedlings that are about 3 inches tall and have leaves, move them to a deeper container so they have room to grow. If you have planted seeds in a container you are going to use, your job is done. Just move them into position.

Chapter 21

CARING FOR YOUR CONTAINER GARDEN

B eginning container gardeners, expert gardeners, or master gardeners; it doesn't matter. There are specific tips you need to follow to keep your container garden looking awesome all season long.

Double container (urbanext.illinois.edu)

Make sure the draining is adequate. Keeping your plants adequately watered, but not drowning is a matter of life and death of a plant. If there aren't enough holes for water to drain out of your pot, the soil becomes too wet and the roots rot. Drill or punch holes in your pot if you need. Adding gravel, shards or stones to the bottom of your container garden does not increase drainage. Unless you are the perfect container gardener caretaker, you need drainage holes.

- Check out the light. Place your container (without plants) where you want it to grow and watch how much sun hits it. Then plant the plants that either love lots of sun or move your pot to a shadier space.

- Potting soil has no accessible nutrients for plants. You need to add those nutrients. You need to add fertilizer directly to your soil. Use a slow release fertilizer to your potting mix. Mix up a big batch in a bucket or fill or pot with soil and mix in the fertilizer. Organic potting soil and organic fertilizers used together are the best. Fertilize every week or two with a liquid fertilizer. Fish emulsion seaweed blend is perfect. It might smell terrible, but plants love it.

- Before you run off to the nursery to buy plants make a list. Greenhouses are wonderful places, but they are also overwhelming. If you find yourself just standing in the doorway wondering what plants you want, you will be there for hours and the joy of planting will have to wait. You should know where you are placing your pots. Head for the sun plants, or the shade plants. If really get into a bind, ask a nursery worker.

- Save the plant tag. Tags let you know how big your plant will grow, how much light and water it needs or when to fertilize. The tag also tells you if your plant is annual or perennial. Tags also give you information about a plants traits or how it is shaped and how it will grow.

- Don't cry if your plants die. Sometimes they do. Known when to give up on a plant in a container. When a plant starts looking sick you can cut it back dramatically and hope for the best. May plants just need a haircut and will grow back wonderfully. However if you have a plant with signs of disease, take it out and put in a new plant. This is why nurseries are open all summer … so you can replant.

- Harden or acclimate your plants. This is a tedious process, but it will help your plants thrive. Move them gradually into the sun, water them sparingly, and expose them to the elements over a period of time.

Chapter 22

Dealing with Container Garden Problems

Container gardening is very popular and there are so many ways you can plant a container garden within your available space. When you first plant or buy your container garden it is awesome, beautiful and perfect. However, plant space is so tight in a container garden; there is less margin for error. Take care of problems as they crop up instead of just hoping planting issues will go away. (Don't just add water and fertilizer to an overcrowded container. Prune, pull, and replant those plants that are looking strangled.)

Common Problems

Tall and spindly plants with little or no production of flowers or vegetables is a problem caused by insufficient light. You may need to augment the sunlight with artificial lighting. If possible, move the container into a sunny spot.

Container garden growing, well, ugly. (www.organizedclutter.net)

Stunted vegetable plants are distressing and if this problem appears in your container garden you may have a low level of phosphate in the soil. Change to a fertilizer with a high phosphate level to correct this problem. Phosphate will help your plants bloom in a limited space.

Plants in a container garden may appear listless and wilted. The problems may be as simple as insufficient watering. Additional watering may help the plants bloom and produce. You may also have inadequate drainage in the soil causing the roots of your plants to get too much water. Check to ensure that the drainage holes in the container are not clogged or blocked with sediment.

Plants in a container garden can appear yellow. If they do, this is excess moisture in your container garden. Re-evaluate the amount of water at scheduled waterings, and check the drainage holes in the container. Make a note of your fertilizing schedule. Inadequate fertilization also causes yellow leaves.

Chapter 23

MISTAKES TO AVOID

As easy and wonderful as container gardening can be, you can do things that will cause you to regret your decision to garden in a container.

Don't add soil and plants to your large container if you are planning to move it to a different spot. One you have filled a container with dirt and plants, it will be overwhelmingly heavy. Place your large pot in the same place where it will live and then plant it. Your back will thank you.

Avoid over watering and drowning your plants. Use containers that have drainage holes. You can never have too many drainage holes. Measure the moisture requirements for your plants and follow directions to the tea. Before you water, check if the soil is moist. If you over water the leaves of your plants may turn yellow and fall off or your plants could get very limp. You can move your container garden into a sheltered spot to dry out if you need.

Coleus, eaten and starving (www.corgnaizedclutter.net)

Avoid under watering. Container gardens need water at least once a day in the heat of the summer. If you have hanging plants or small containers they may need to be watered twice a day. These types of container gardens hold less soil and thus less moisture. Really soak your plants, but again don't drown them.

One annoying mistake that is awkward is plant to pot ratio. Consider the proportions of your plants to the container. A large container filled with short plants will look silly. Try to plant at least one plant that is as tall as the container. Use plants that spill over the sides. Experiment but don't keep all the plants the same size.

When purchasing plants for your container garden, look for healthy plants. Go to a reputable local nursery to start your quest for healthy plants. Box stores may have awesome plants, but they might be diseased and unhealthy. Ask the gardener if they will help you pick out appropriate plants for you container garden.

When your container garden starts to look leggy, and it will, cut plants back. If they are looking too tired and overdone, put them in an out-of-the-way spot until they rebound. Give them a good haircut and they will be healthy and happy.

Don't starve your plants. Potting mixes have very few nutrients that plants need. Add those nutrients to the soil. Read labels. Use fertilizers for flowers plants on ornamentals. Vegetables and herbs require their own special types of fertilizers.

Avoid having unrealistic expectations. When planning a container garden, think about what you are doing in the summer. If you travel quite a bit get self-watering containers or an automatic drip system. It is always a good idea to garden how you live. If you are formal you may want to plant container gardens in specific ways and colors. If you are casual, just plant how you like. Most container gardeners love big and overflowing containers with lot of colors and blossoms. Grow vegetables and herbs galore in a container garden. The best advice from gardeners is to have fun with however you garden.

Repotting

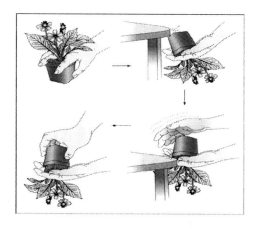

Indoor kitchen garden (www.allmodern,com)

*Correct technique for removing a pant from
its pot (www.dummies.com)*

Most healthy container garden plants outgrow their posts. All you need to do to reinvigorate a root bound plant is to repot it in a bigger pot.

Recognize when it is time to repot. If soil drains out quickly or is degraded, roots protrude from drainage holes, and water sits on the soil surface too long after watering are a few of the signs that say, "re-pot me." Think a plant looks top heavy or as if it is going to break the pot? Get a bigger pot.

The best time to repot most plants is when they are growing in the spring or summer. But if you are a gardener who schedules repotting and repots in the fall, that is great, too.

- Get the plant out of its pot. Water the root ball thoroughly in advance. Invert the pot and support the top of the root ball with your hand. Literally pull the root ball and plant out of the smaller pot. You may have to knock the edge of the pot against a sturdy surface. Be careful not to break your pot.

- The plant ready for reporting should slid out with the root ball and soil in one piece. If soil falls free of the roots, you may not need to repot. Look for white or light colored roots. If you have black or foul smelling roots, these are signs of fungal diseases. Unless you are terribly attached to the plant, you might want to put it on the compost heap.

- Trim the roots and loosen up the root ball before replanting. A sharp knife or pruning shears are perfect for this job. Make about three or four vertical cuts a third of the way up the root ball. If you have roots growing in a circular pattern, cut through them. This will prevent the plant from strangling itself. Roots that are thick along the sides of the root ball need to be shaved or peeled away. Gently untangle the root ball with your fingers.

- To prevent soil from leaking out the bottom of the new pot, cover the drainage hole with a coffee filter or pot shard. Don't use gravel or charcoal in the bottom of pots. They really don't help with drainage and do take up valuable space. Make sure the pot is slightly bigger than the root ball.

- Fill with fresh potting soil and trim the top of the plant. Put a few inches of moist soil in the pot and tap it down. Plant the plant the center of the pot, and look to see if the root ball is sitting about an inch below the rim of the pot. If the plant is in the pot too deep, raise it and add more soil. If the root ball is too high, dig out some soil, or just start over.

- Fill the space around the root ball with soil. Stuff or press soil in around the plants. If you are a filler, just fill the pot to the brim and let the soil settle in during watering. Always leave some room at the top of the pot so it can hold water.

Chapter 24

INDOOR CONTAINER GARDENS

Grow awesome flowers in an indoor container garden (www2.fiskars.com)

Nothing brightens up your home than a container garden. Use spring bulbs and for a totally wonderful spring pick-me up. Let the glorious colors and textures of your favorite flowers become key elements of your home's décor.

Bring spring indoors by pairing up Dutch hyacinths, trumpet daffodils, pink tulips and grape hyacinths in a metal or ceramic container. Find something awesome and eclectic at a flea market or antique store and just plant your heart away. Pack blubs close together to intensify their ambience. Top off your living arrangement with green moss.

Succulents are very popular and you can go wild with them in a complementary pot. Cacti have thorns, but find those that are soft and inviting. Choose tall cacti to anchor your pot and small ones to emphasize. Succulents do grow very fast, but are very awesome. Use Kalanchoe thyrsiflora, spaghetti strap agave or hope peperoni. You can find succulent potting mix at garden stores. Never use the soil from your ground garden for a succulent container garden. Garden soil contains harmful bacteria.

Figure 2 Fun indoor tomato container garden (yourorganicchild.co)

A woodsy mossy basket can hold a lush growth of plants straight out of the woodland. Doily lace cap hydrangea blooms added with bold baby ferns and vines spilling over the edge of the container are perfect for any sunny spot in your home.

Terrariums and glass plant houses are making a comeback. They are endearing, easy to take care of and just wonderful to look at. Try a rex begonia, white Anne fittonia and mosses you found on a walk, and add them to a stunning glass house or bowl. You won't regret what you have created! Just remember to mist them once a week.

Wine-colored fall container Echeveria nodulosa, Phormium "Sundowner", and Heucherella or Sweet Tea. (www.sunset.com)

Give your indoor container garden good air circulation. Pay attention to their needs and they will be happy. Take care of pest problems immediately and get to know your plants. Plants need food, water and sunlight to survive, but different plants require different treatments. Choose houseplants that thrive on the amount of light you provide. Healthy plants will ward of pests and diseases better than sick or weak plants.

Use regular fertilizer to maintain healthy growth. An all-around fertilizer can be added to your watering can. Use a fertilizer that is a balanced formula of 6-12-6 fertilizer plus humic and amino acids.

Add vitamins. Fertilize house container gardens from January through September and then let them rest.

Have a watering schedule. If you alternate periods of drought and flood you will stress out your plant's root system. Most plants like moist roots, but are not fond of wet soils. You might have plants that prefer to dry out between waterings, but always check the care label. Indoor plant books will also help you determine the right watering schedule. Invest in self-watering planters to make it easier to keep your plants happily hydrated.

Us a good natural and multipurpose pest control spray. Neem oil spray is a natural potassium pest control spray and works on a wide variety of pests. It will kill scale on your houseplants and controls powdery mildew.

Indoor herb and vegetable garden (www.southernsavers.com)

Chapter 25

10 CONTAINER GARDEN IDEAS

So many different ways to display your container gardens. You can group them, use them alone, or place them in our ground garden. Add container gardens to your porch or use them as a welcome mat. Anyway you choose will be awesome. Browse through these ten ideas to get an idea of what you can do with a container garden.

Wander your local garden store, pick out the plants you love and then go for the container. Let the container extend the theme. A container garden is an instant garden.

Match icy blue plans together with warm combos of bright pinks and purples. Organize your container garden in threes for the best design. That means three containers with three plants each or one plant in three containers. Keep the sizes relevant.

Start out with a thriller, add a filler, and finish with a spiller. Gorgeous containers include calla lilies, foliage or flowering plants like lantana and geraniums, and a training plants like Livingstone daisy. Let it cascade over the edge for a gorgeous arrangement.

Sunshine Garden (www.midwestliving.com)

Figure 3 Gorgeous! Lush Container Garden
(www.midwestliving.com)

Nothing speaks drama like this awesome Sunshine in a container garden. Plants that love the sun give your yard pizazz. Use vinca vine, water hyssop, annual phlox, daisies, impatiens (New Guinea), bellflower, White monkey flower, Lobela, Gerbera Daisy, Mandevilla vine, Delphinium, Dusty Miller and Salvia (Blue Queen.) All these plants can be found in your local greenhouse they are well known and grow well in many climate zones.

Vegetables grown in bright pots to add
pizazz and interest (www.bhg.com)

Check out gardening books, catalogues and green houses. Container gardening using vegetables is becoming more and more popular. You can grow your own food in fantastic containers. Try this awesome container garden of tomatoes. An increasing number of compact and dwarf varieties are being developed for small spaces.

Cherry tomatoes and basil in a hanging basket (www.bhg.com)

Pair tomato and basil together. This is a very pretty display and will be very tasty when used in your favorite Italian recipe. If you are container gardening using hanging plants, you might want to design a drip system. This is the same type os system that cities use to keep their hanging gardens gorgeous all year. Check with a garden supply store.

Get creative! Use recycled wooden boxes or anything else you have hanging around for this container garden (www.bhg.com)

Save money by using recycled containers. Old wine crates or milk boxes create an eclectic and colorful container garden. Lettuce sits side by side with Thumbelina carrots, overbearing strawberries and marigolds (yes, marigolds are eatable).

Anything that can hold soil can be a container garden. This awesome container garden is a living centerpiece that can go outside or indoors.

Modern look, using aluminum garbage cans. It might be bet to purchase new cans that haven't been used (Courtesy of Brian Patrick Flynn)

How to Grow Practically Everything

@2010 Dorling Kindersley Limited

Just use whatever you have around to plant a container garden. New aluminum garbage cans filled with spider plants and taller salvia and vining pansies make an impression against the brick of this home. Notice the containers are on wheels for ease of moving. If you are using containers this large, note that using plastic bottles as inside drainage instead of rocks will keep things light and moveable.

Really neat carry-along succulents can be moved anywhere you want. An old metal tool toe makes a perfect home for these succulents. Drill drainage holes in the boot, don't overwater and enjoy. Plant with different types of succulents.

Drawers and shelving as a container garden (themicrogardener.com)

4www.diynetwork.com

Recycle your old furniture by turning it into a container garden. You can do just about anything you like if you have imagination. Wooden drawers set on a ladder framework forms a great space for a container garden.

Chapter 26

TIPS FOR SUCCESSFUL CONTAINER GARDENING

- Purchase sterilized soil for use in your containers. This will ensure the potting soil is free from weed seeds and diseases.

- Look out for weeds such as the onion weed and yellow nutsedge. One these weeds are established they are almost impossible to get rid of.

- Grouping garden pots is better and more effective visually and practically than scattering containers around your yard.

- Water late in the afternoon when evaporation is less.

- Add fertilizer and plant foods tick on a scheduled basis.

- Repot plants when they outgrow the container.

- Choose the right size container for your pot plants. If you are using large pots, first choose where you want them to reside, and then fill with soil and plants. Carting spoil-filled containers is not easy.

- Use organic mulch to discourage weed growth and encourage surface roots.

Any container will work! (www.landscape-and-garden.com)

Plants are light sensitive. Before moving your plants from a shady to a sunny location, prepare them by moving them gradually. This will "toughen" up your plants and prevent sun burn.

Chapter 27

URBAN HOMESTEADING

Urban homesteading, frugal living, living green, and an environmentally friendly existence are terms for an age where people are trying to provide more for themselves and rely less on commercialization. Bartering with neighbors is the new social media, and fixing dinner from your own backyard garden is the new gourmet cooking. Being more self-sufficient, so you don't have to rely on anyone else to take care of your family, might seem impossible in today's world of "too much to do in one day." There are so many ways to bring homesteading into your life without upsetting your schedule.

Living a simple, self-reliant living is very "trendy", so what does it really mean. Urban homesteading is the movement of urbanites who are growing their own food, creating a barnyard in their backyard, and canning the fruits of their labors. It's all about taking a deep breath, stepping backward and living a more purposeful life. It is living a simple life in the city environment surrounded by all the modern conveniences you have come to expect.

Urban homesteading is transforming your city or suburban home into a property that produces some of its own food and other needs. Homestead and seek self-sufficiency, creating a home with the goal of reducing environmental impact. Returning to a home-based family centered on frugal and responsible living.

The current trend to urban homesteading is a positive drift. It is a social, conscious and a real lifestyle choice. Homesteading in the city requires responsibility to your neighbors and fellow citizens. It will bring you rich rewards if you go about it in an accountable and positive manner.

Urban homesteading will always be a work in progress, but the current, positive trend in living in a self-sustained society has several factors that make up the ideal urban homesteading lifestyle:

Grow more than 50% of your diet, organically, on an urban lot. This lot should be less than half an acre and include visually appealing landscaping.

- Use alternative energy sources. These are solar and wind that create energy efficiency.

- Use substitute fuels and transportation including bio-fuels, bike, walk or taking public transportation.

- Raise farm animals for food and fertilizer. You will need to contact your city offices for the regulations on having farm animals in your yard.

- To live an urban homestead life, practice waste reduction. Use it, wear it out, and make it do, go without, compost it, or re-purpose it. You might want to forget going to the trendy boutiques and purchasing ready-to-wear clothing. Waste reduction means mending tears in pants, darning socks, hand-me-downs, and dressing simple. It also means doing your own laundry, composting your kitchen waste, and turning worn out goods into something else.

- Practice water conservation and recovery. Water recovery includes reclaiming gray water and collecting rainwater.

- Live simply or in the manner of past eras. Find your talent for homemaking skills including food preservation and preparation. Make your own cheese, butter and bread.

- Learn to do home and vehicle maintenance and repairs. Take a carpentry class so that you can do home repairs and basic construction.

- Develop a home-based economy and earn a living from the land or find work you can do at home. How weird would it be to go to the office in the city in a suit and tie, then come home, put on coveralls, and jump into skinning chickens?

- Always be a good neighbor. Ask yourself, who would I want to live next to me? Offer a healing hand, let the neighbors see what you are doing. Urban homesteading is a community-based way of life. Encourage your neighbors to join in your endeavors to be self-sufficient (urbanhomestead.org).

Chapter 28

Urban vs. Rural Homesteading

Permaculture Center - food garden programs (www.sprig.co.za)

Trend: Farm animals in your urban back-

yard (www.hgtvgardens.com)

Urban homesteading, in a nutshell, is living "country" in the city. Rural homesteading, on the other hand, IS country living, a continual journey and a purpose toward a sustainable and self-sufficient life. Both urban and rural homesteading is a work in progress. Take it slow and easy and don't stress about the little things that don't come together perfectly.

Permaculture

Part of an urban way of living is permaculture that is a design approach used to relate edible and sustainable landscapes. These landscapes are designed to work with nature. Take it one step more and create a balance with how the environment should really look.

The goal of urban homesteading and permaculture is to create a self-sustaining system using few, but natural resources. Permaculture goes a bit further and strives to balance living with nature. Permaculture is eliminating the use of chemical pesticides and allowing native beneficial insects to tend the garden. Using native plants in the landscape, creating a productive yard for people and nourishing the natural environment are goals of permaculture.

Permaculture, coined in the mid-70s by David Holmgren and Bill Mollison, principles are designed to show people how to design a rich and sustainable way of life. Landscapes are calculated to save water, energy and soil nutrients. The permaculture gardener gives back time, energy, and the environment by letting animals and plants to do their thing.

There are three rules to permaculture. One is taking are of the Earth, next take care of the people who live on the Earth, and three, share the surplus with those around you.

Begin your permaculture design by looking at your landscape for things you regularly use but could replace with more ecological versions. Maybe you should replace your grass lawns with a native ground cover that promotes pollination and bees. Install a rainwater catchment system to reduce city water use. Compost kitchen and yard waste and return what you have grown and eaten back to the earth.

Permaculture is a way to make your bit of land productive, simple and fun. Sit down to a meal that you prepared exclusively with ingredients from your yard.

Live with the Earth, not just existing on it. (www.eco-evolution.com)

Permaculture binds with urban homesteading and focuses on long-term sustainability and self-sufficiency. It teaches farming methods that improve crop yields. You have a system of education designed to improve health and the quality of life, you learn to be cooperative with groups as well as nature, and permaculture strives to improve housing and public spaces.

Chapter 29

HOMESTEADING AS A LIFESTYLE CHOICE

Homesteading is becoming a more accepted way of life throughout the world. The times are uncertain, and the economy is uneasy and many families are working toward being self-sufficient. You can also call homesteading frugal living, getting back to basics and living off the land.

Homesteading is not about removing yourself from traditional society, but engaging yourself in finding solutions to self-sufficient living. The challenge of frugal living can be fulfilling and at the same time difficult. Most people, however, who have embraced homesteading lifestyles find they are more energized and benefit physically from a stronger connection to labor. The keys to homesteading are conserving resources, staying focused and being grounded in the most important things in life – family, self-sufficiency, and happiness.

Homesteading is the desire for the best possible nutrition. Homesteading is raising your own natural foods from organic tomatoes and grass-fed cows to pigs and chickens fed natural diets. The health benefits make this a very worthwhile lifestyle.

It is living off the land and teaching others to live a more frugal and environmentally friendly life.

Chapter 30

STARTING YOUR OWN GARDEN

You are ready to grow your own food and become self-sufficient. It is a bit daunting as you look over the available land you have outside your home, and if you live in an apartment with only a balcony, it can be discouraging. Don't despair! There are tips to planning a garden for self-sufficiency. Just start small and build on it each year. Before long, you will be producing a great deal of food on your own land.

- Grow high-value fruits and vegetables. Plant regular vegetables that taste so much better than store-bought varieties.

- Make use of late winter/early spring and use cold frames, tunnels, and cloches. Using growing techniques will help stretch the season. You can get a head start on growing spring salads by a month if you use covers.

- Extend fall crops by using clothes and plastic to protect them from frost. You can extend the garden season by using more cold-tolerant greens and root crops.

- Even if you are an apartment or condo gardener, take advantage of container and vertical gardening. Grow tomatoes up against your outside wall and use containers that you can move in and out of your home when the weather is too cold. One apartment complex nearby has a tenant who artistically grows her vegetables on the balcony using containers that are colorful and artistic. She has a tremendous garden all year round because she employs the proper techniques of planting, watering and fertilizing.

- Plant June bearing strawberries and early raspberries. In the fall take advantage of late-ripening raspberries and apples.

- Grow what is suggested for your climate. Soil type also determines what grows where you live. If you cannot grow beets, but carrots are your specialty, then grow carrots and trade for beets.

- Grow your own mint, sage, raspberry leaf and nettles to make healthy teas. You can use rhubarb stalk to make a tea that tastes remarkably like lemonade. You can easily make your own sodas, wine and hard ciders from berries and fruits.

- Perennials come back year after year, and this saves you time and money. Asparagus, rhubarb, Jerusalem artichokes, horseradish, plus bunching onions are perennial.

- Try not to spend all summer growing something that is not a crop in your area. Nothing is more frustrating to a gardener who is trying to grow watermelon and cantaloupes, and finds the soil, temperature and growing season is just not conducive.

- An herb garden with dill, rosemary, basil, sage and parsley is wonderful and can be grown indoors as well as outdoors. Saves money on purchasing expensive freeze dried herbs from the grocery store.

- Don't over plant one type of vegetable or fruit. Some gardeners go overboard on the tomatoes, squash and cucumbers. Of course, if you are really self-sufficient you can sell your excess at fall farmer's markets.

- Try growing something new every year.

- Growing your own garden is a noble goal. Take it one step at a time if you are new to gardening and build it up every year. To be a true homesteader, don't give up!

Starting a garden (www.gardenguides.com)

Consider where you are going to plant your garden. Scout out the soil condition of your garden. If you have pretty good soil, you are lucky, but most urban gardeners have awful soil. Urban soils usually lack in organic matter and have limestone and clays that come from the construction of your home. If you hit little rocks when you dig and dig up tons of dried out clay, you will find that you do need a great deal of compositing and supplement soil help. Consider the rainfall. If you have inconsistent rainfall, you will need to set up an irrigation system. Choose plants that are drought tolerant and yet can handle rain deluges.

Love wildlife? Plant your flower and vegetable gardens for wildlife benefits. Pollinators benefit with nourishing flowers or edible berries or seeds. Hollies and pyracantha produce fruits that bird eat to get them through the winter months. Coneflowers and other perennials produce seeds that provide meals for birds.

Think about the overall aesthetic quality of your garden. The looks and potential of your land might be what gets you looking at gardening in the beginning. You want a yard that looks awesome. Contrasting foliage with flowers, adding vegetables to your flower gardens and creating a backdrop of berries are factors to consider when you are contemplating a garden for aesthetic value or even self-sufficiency value.

Chapter 31

VARIABLES FOR A SURVIVAL GARDEN

Growing a survival garden means incorporating easy to grow vegetables that produce more than one harvest. Vegetable varieties should be the types of vegetables your family will eat. Do not grow vegetables your family absolutely will not tolerate.

Find vegetables that have a high amount of vitamins, minerals, and nutritional value. Use plants that possess medicinal properties. Green vegetables like broccoli, Brussels sprouts, Lima beans, peas, artichokes, cauliflower, asparagus and sweet potatoes are the most nutritious vegetables in the world.

Use plant varieties that grow naturally in your area. Less time and effort will be needed to raise crops if they are native.

If you have limited space, use plants that take up as little space as possible. Vertical gardening is excellent if you have a small yard.

Plant vegetables that are suited for storage. Potatoes, onions and root crops like carrots store well and can be used all year round.

Grow varieties that serve more than one purpose. Root crops or broccoli leaves can be fed to livestock.

Choose the size for your vegetable garden that is conducive to the size of your yard. Pay attention to sun and shade. Plants in your garden will want a south facing venue. Most plants require a minimum of five hours of direct sunlight per day. Watch the path of shadows from trees, tall objects and adjacent buildings in your yard. The maximum continuous light is the best location for your garden.

Consider the proximity to trees. Trees do shade gardens, but they also spread roots. You garden should be at least 10' beyond the drip line of any nearby trees. You may need to dig a barrier around your garden if you need to block root incursions. Do this by digging a narrow trench deeper than existing roots. Set a sheet of galvanized metal roofing or inert heavy materials into the trench. This material should not allow roots to penetrate. Fill the trench with barrier materials to the soil level.

Consider wind exposure. In windy areas, you will need a fence or berm to serve as a wind barrier.

Sloped land needs to be terraced to grow vegetables without losing crops. Beds should be level, or you will have uneven water distribution and erosion. Build up the low side of the sloped land with flat rocks or wood slabs. Fill in with soil and level the beds.

Chapter 32

COMPOST

You cannot say too much about the value of compost to the garden soil. Compost gives nutrient rich humus to soils which in turn fuels plant growth and restores vitality to tired or awful soil. A compost bin is an essential part of your survival vegetable garden. Keep your compost bin or pile sealed to keep flying insects away and to contain smells. You can purchase a nice compost tumbler for around $150. A compost tumbler will speed up the cooking process.

Make your own compost

Managing Fertilizer (www.uri.edu)

Urban compost bin. Nicely done! (www.seattlecentral.edu)

- Carbon rich materials like branches and dried leaves give the compost a light and fluffy texture.

- Nitrogen is protein rich matter that include food scraps, green lawn clippings, and manures.

- Use one-third green and two-thirds brown materials in your compost. Brown matter allows oxygen to penetrate and nourish the organisms that reside in the compost. Make sure you do not have too much nitrogen, or you will have a smelly and slowly decomposing anaerobic mess.

- If you are a serious gardener, practice hot composting. Gather enough materials to make a pile at least three feet deep. Alternate four to eight inch layers of green materials or kitchen scraps, fresh leaves, coffee grounds plus brown materials like dried leaves, shredded paper and sawdust. Sprinkle water over the pile regularly so it is always the consistency of a damp sponge. Try not to add too much water or the microorganisms in your pile will become waterlogged and drown. If this happens your compost pile will rot.

Check the temperature of the pile with a thermometer on a regular basis. You can also just insert your hand into the middle of the pile to check if it is "warm." If the thermometer reads between 130 and 150°F or feels very warm, your compost is ready to turn.

Turn your compost with a garden fork. Stirring the pile helps it "cook" and prevents material from becoming matted down. When the pile no longer gives off heat and is dry, brown and crumbly, it is cooked and ready to use in the garden.

Use worms for your compost. One gardener in a nearby urban neighborhood has a three foot square wire cage that is lined with newspaper and peat moss. Purchased red wigglers are thrown into the cage. Add your household and lawn scraps and by spring you will have an unbelievable wonderful compost. This type of compost grows just about anything. The red wrigglers love squash, pumpkins, and melons. Ask your neighbors for their green waste, especially pumpkins, and the red wrigglers will turn these vegetables into awesome compost within a matter of weeks.

Chapter 33

FERTILIZERS

Use cow or horse manure as a good source of organic material. The manure should be well aged, so it is not "hot" and burns tender transplants. However, do be aware that manure will contain many weed seeds. You can cover the manure with mulch to help block sunlight from reaching weed seeds to help keep the weed invaders down.

Green manure is from the legume family of plants. It can be chopped up and spaded into the soil for your garden. Green compost adds organic substances and readily grows into humus. Green manure compost are planted in the fall and ploughed into the soil in early spring.

Rain Barrel (www.est.edu)

You can also augment your garden with sea soil. Garden centers carry sea soil that is a combination of fish by-products and sawdust. It is rich in mineral and vital nutrients and can be applied directly to your garden beds.

You may also need to amend your soil with bone meal, blood meal, and a variability of amendments that address your soil wants. Glacial rock dust is good as a soil amendment. Rock dust is organic, slow releasing and loaded with essential nutrients that plants love. It encourages the root systems of trees, lawns, flower and shrub beds as well as vegetable gardens.

The final touch to prepare you garden is to level the soil and rake it smooth. Level and smooth ground helps with the uniform water absorption from rains and encourages sprouting.

Mulch the paths between your beds. Dirt clods can fall into the pathways, and that brings up weeds. Scrape away grass or surface weeds and cover your pathways with two layers of landscape cloth. Then cover with a layer of bark mulch. Mulch will keep weeds away from pathways and from migrating into vegetable beds.

Once you have set and soiled your bed, do not step in the beds. You will not need to get into the bed plus stepping on the beds will compress the soil and reduce aeration. Lay a plank across your beds for walking on if you must go from one side to the other.

Chapter 34

COLLECTING THE RAIN

Homesteading and being self-sufficient means you use all the resources you have available. This includes collecting rainwater. With a little ingenuity you can collect rain water in any container that will hold water. The major criteria for collecting rain water is your container must have a mesh screen to prevent mosquito breeding.

The most efficient set up is a rain barrel with an open top underneath a gutter downspout. This will catch the rainwater runoff from your roof. Commercial rain barrels can hold about 50 gallons of water and some commercial models come pre-equipped with a hose attachment.

Natural rainwater is perfect for survival gardens. Rain water is not processed like your tap water and doesn't contain the minerals found in wells or the chlorine in municipal supplies. You can also use rain water to wash your car, do the laundry or even take a shower.

Watering lawns and gardens can consume almost 40 percent of the total household water use during a growing season. A simple rain barrel system utilizing collected water for outdoor use can have a huge effect on becoming self-reliant. You will save on water bills and reduce the energy used to process and purify water for your outdoor watering needs.

Chapter 35

How to Build a Rain Collection System

The most commons rain collection systems includes one or more rain barrels between 40 to 80 gallons each and located below gutter downspouts. This will gather rain water from the roof. You can then attach a drip irrigation system or hose to the spigot valves at the bottom of the rain barrel.

Plastic ran barrel kits can be purchased at home centers for about $100. If you would rather do it yourself, you can make your own rain barrel for about half the cost. Purchase a large waterproof container, like plastic trash cans with snap-on lids. You can purchase wood barrels from wineries, or you can obtain a 55-gallon barrel from a bulk food supplier. If you purchase a used barrel clean it out to make sure that it does not contain any compounds that could be harmful to plants, animals, or humans. If you don't know what was in a barrel, don't use it. Purchase a barrel that is opaque. Light can cause algae growth.

Barrels of water are the perfect breeding grounds for mosquitos and a great incubator for algae. Filters and screens over the barrel openings should prevent insect infestations, but do add one tablespoon of vegetable oil to the water in the barrel. This will coat the top surface and deprive mosquito larvae of oxygen.

Chapter 36

DIY Rain Barrel System

- Barrel
- Spade bit for a drill
- Jigsaw and a hole saw
- Barb fitting with nut for overflow hose
- 1 1/2" sump drain hose for overflow
- 3⁄4" hose sillcock
- 3⁄4" male pipe coupling
- 3⁄4" bulkhead connector
- Pliers
- Window screening
- Cargo strap with ratchet

- Teflon tape

- Silicone caulk

1. Cut a large opening in the barrel top. Mark the size and shape of your barrel opening Drill a starter hole, and then cut out the shape with a jigsaw.

2. Drill a hole near the top of the barrel for the overflow fitting. This is the overflow hose. Thread the fitting into the hole and secure it to the barrel on the inside using a retainer nut and rubber washer. Slide the overflow hose into the barbed end of the barb elbow until the end of the hose seats against the elbow flange.

3. Drill the access hole for the spigot.

4. Tighten the stem of the sillcock onto a threaded coupling inserted into the access hole. Inside the barrel, a rubber washer is slipped onto the coupling end and then a threaded bushing is tightened over the coupling to create a seal. Apply a strip of Teflon tape to all threaded parts before making each connection. Caulk around the spigot with clear silicone caulk.

5. Screen over the opening in the top of the barrel. Lay a piece of fiberglass insect mesh over the top of the trash can and secure it around the rim with a cargo strap or bungee cord

that can be drawn drum-tight. Snap the trash can lid over the top. Once you have installed the rain barrel, periodically remove and clean the mesh.

Chapter 37

HOW TO INSTALL A RAIN BARREL

Rain barrels collecting systems can be purchased, made from a kit, or one you designed yourself. How well you system works depends on where you place the barrel(s). Your system can be just a temporary one that holds rain water and directs it to your yard through a hose. You can use your rain barrels as reservoirs to supply water on-demand when you need to fill up watering cans. or buckets. If you rain barrel spigot is the main ways you dispense water, elevate the rain barrel off the ground on a base for easier access.

Whenever you can, place your rain barrel system in a shaded area. Sunlight causes algae growth if you barrel system is partially translucent.

Tools and Materials Needed

- *Screwdriver* (possibly a drill)

- *Hack saw*

- *Rain barrel*

- *Hose & fittings*

- *Base material, pavers, bricks or gravel*

- *Downspout adapter and extension*

- *Teflon tape*

1. Locate your barrel under a downspout and as close to the area you want to irrigate. Place your barrel on stable ground.

2. Install the spigot. (Tip: You can purchase kits that have a second spigot for filling watering cans.) Use Teflon tape at all threaded fittings for a tight seal. Attach the overflow tube. Install your overflow tube away from the foundation of your home.

3. Use a hacksaw to cut the downspout to length. Connect the elbow fitting to the downspout using sheet-metal screws. Cover the top of the rain barrel. There are systems that have a cover made from wire mesh and the water is delivered

directly though the mesh. Other system have an opening directly in the top of the barrel to gather the rain.

4. Attach the downspout to the rain barrel with flexible downspout extensions. Attach to the elbow and the barrel cover.

5. Connect the drip irrigation tube or garden hose to the spigot. A Y-fitting allows you to feed the drip irrigation system through a garden hose when the rain barrel is empty.

6. Increase water storage by connecting two or more rain barrels together. You can purchase a linking kit at home gardening stores.

Chapter 38

Types of Homestead Gardening

Homestead gardening is not just survival gardening and turning your landscape into a vegetable field. It is living frugally and healthy by growing your plants in any way possible. Use container gardening, rooftop gardening, and square foot and vertical gardening. Try your hand at circular gardening. Live self-sufficient anywhere and anyway you can.

Chapter 39

CONTAINER AND CIRCULAR GARDENING

Circular gardening can be defined as pint-sized portable plots and can also be called container gardens. These circular or container gardens can be taken anywhere you move, and circular gardening pots are specifically designed to grow vegetables.

You need a good spot with at least six to eight hours of sunlight during the day. It would be best if you did not keep your circular garden right next to your house. You could end up with too much shade and too little air circulation. Air is important to keep away the fungal growth and related diseases. Try to avoid damp spots near down pipes, too.

Vegetables growing in a container www.vegetablegardener.com

Types of crops you can grow in a circular garden are tomatoes, onions, carrots, peas, broccoli, and cauliflower.

Try container gardening if you live in an apartment or have a small yard. Container gardening is the best way to grow plants that have specific garden soil requirements or if you live in a dry and arid area. Watering container gardens is so much easier and economical than trying to water an entire row garden.

Advantages to container gardening include:

- You control the amount of water and food that the plants receive.

- Water conservation is practiced since you are only watering a small space.

- Control the types of soil where the plants are grown.

- Localize and target spaces to place plants for gardening.

- Containers can be the focal point in your garden and add distinction to certain areas. Containers are also made to complement your garden – flower or vegetable.

- Group pots and pot plants together to create a lush tropical look or to blend different types of vegetables.

- Use container gardening as a screening tactic. Plant your containers with tall plants to ensure privacy.

- Reuse you pots at the end of the season.

- You can just use about anything to grow flowers, fruits, and vegetables and call it a container.

Container gardening is perfect for growing dwarf fruit trees. Group your dwarf trees together to encourage pollination, privacy and to grow awesome fruit crops.

You can use typical potting soil or a soil mix in your containers, or better yet, use your own homemade compost. If you are purchasing potting soil, purchase the best quality you can afford. Good quality potting soil gives your plants nourishment. The health of your plants does depend on the soil.

Potting Mix Recipe

- Seven parts good garden loam soil for nutrients.

- Three parts of thoroughly decomposed compost or peat moss for nutrient additives and water retention.

- Two parts well-aged manure for nutrients.

- Two parts river sand for drainage.

- Add to this mix 125 ml or half a cup of bone meal or super phosphate. Include 125 ml of a general fertilizer as well as a level teaspoon of agricultural lime.

Wash out your pots from last year and soak terracotta or clay pots. If you pre-soak your garden terracotta pots, they will not absorb moisture from the potting soil or compost. If you do not soak your pots, the soil will shrink away from the sides of the pot, and the result is a gap where water will run off and leave the middle of the pot dry.

Make sure you have drainage holes in your container or circular pots. A minimum of four holes to 1 cm of each pot is a good measurement. Drainage holes should be covered with shards of terracotta, or you can cover the holes with a cloth. Do not block the drainage holes. Place a layer of river sand over the hole covers to prevent the drainage holes from becoming blocked. The river sand should be no thicker than 3 cm.

Add manufactured water-retaining granules to potting soils to hold water. Fill the container with soil to accommodate the root ball of the plant. Remove the plant from its host, carefully fit the plant into the container, fill it up with soil and press down. Tip: water your plant well just before potting it.

Carrots grown in a container

Make sure you water the pot plants regularly. Add a layer or organic compost to keep the soil moist. If you are planting seedlings from the greenhouse, move them in stages until they can tolerate direct sunlight.

Chapter 40

ROOFTOP GARDENING

Rooftop gardening has been practiced for centuries. City dwellers tuck plants on roofs and fire escapes to provide home-grown vegetables and provide garden space. Roof top gardens are gaining popularity in residential communities, as well as commercial sites as more apartment, and urban dwellers become aware of homesteading and frugal living.

Gorgeous urban rooftop garden (sites.google.com)

Consider a roof top gardening if you need to make use of unused or underused space. A rooftop garden also has these elements:

- Beautifies an eyesore

- Provides privacy

- Environmentally friendly

- Good sun exposure

- No roaming pests like deer, gophers, or rodents

Fully planted green rooftops or where you completely cover the roof with soil and plants can be great environmentally but is difficult to maintain. If you are contemplating this type of garden, you may need to hire a structural engineer or architect to make sure the structure will hold heavy soil, plants and the water that is needed.

Use containers and raised beds, instead. You can create your own special rooftop garden with containers. Containers are perfect for rooftop gardens; they are portable, light, flexible and very affordable.

Maintaining container plants on a rooftop are like taking care of containers on the ground. You do need to consider these ideas before for you start your rooftop garden:

- Permission is necessary. You must check with your landlord or building code. Make sure you have good accessibility and fire regulations allow you to grow containers on the roof. You do not want firefights to stumble over you containers if they are not aware they are there neither do you want to get to the roof via a fire escape.

- Can you get water to the roof? Watering can become difficult to carry up a ladder and containers do require a lot of water. You might install a rain barrel system and use drip irrigation from the water barrel.

- Look for sun exposure. You may think you have plenty of sun on the roof, but are you shaded by nearby buildings? Be careful you do not have too much sun. You don't want your plants to swelter on the top of a concrete roof.

- Heat could be a problem. Ambient heat is reflected from the roof surface and the buildings around you.

- Wind is a factor. It can whip down straight urban streets and high-rises. Consider a wall or fencing to use as a windbreak.

- Privacy is a question if you have neighboring buildings. If your rooftop garden is in full view, consider screening. Use umbrella tables, trellises, or become friends with the people in the next building.

Park-like rooftop urban garden (www.lifegreensystems.com

Request an area for storage. You will need to keep your tools, compost, buckets, and fertilizer in a convenient space. You may want to use bench seating with built in storage.

Chapter 41

SQUARE FOOT GARDENING

To turn the concrete jungle in your backyard into an urban homesteading experience, use square foot gardening. It is easy, and the crops you produce will help you be self-sufficient.

Square foot gardening boxes. (beforeitsnews.com)

How to Build Your Boxes

Materials

- 2'x4' boxes

- 3 1"x6"x10' lumber

- Decking screws

- Covering for the bottom of the boxes

- Screws

- Soil or home grown compost, newspaper

- Starter plants or seeds.

Tools Need

- Saw

- Industrial Stapler

- Electric Screw Driver to make the job go much faster and easier.

Putting your gardening box together (www.instructables.com)

Add your compost, newspaper and leaves or other organic materials. Dump in your special soil mixtures and beginning adding marks along the edges of your garden box. Mark off 1' increments. These are the "helps" to you square feet planting areas.

Create a grid using string, purchased grid markers, or wood slats. Grab your plants and start planting. Plant according to plant's direction. The direction on the seedlings will tell you to plant every 12" apart or one plant in each square area. Follow these instructions, so you do not crowd your vegetables.

VERTICAL GARDENING

Growing vegetables vertically and in an urban
environment. (www2.fiskars.com)

Urban vertical gardening can be very creative. You can use
ready-made products or get creative and make your own
vertical garden containers. Almost any plant will grow in a suitably
sized container. Just remember when you are building a vertical

container system you are not limited to conventional pots and trellises. Anything that can hold soil and drain adequately will work.

Wall hanging pots are perfect for urban homesteading vertical gardening. Miniature terracotta clay pots and old tin #10 cans hung on the wall using large pipe clamps, or other techniques are perfect. Place dozens of small pots on a wall in a pattern and you have an excellent vertical garden.

Pallets can be used to grow vegetables vertically. Take the pallets apart, build shelving and customize your container to accommodate vertical planting. Recycled bicycle rims, or use hangings on a fence, post or wall. Browse through your yard and see what you have to use as a vertical container hung on a wall. You can use eye-catching pot hangers to hang terra cotta pots on a post, wall or fence. These hangers can be used to form a multitiered garden of chard, kohlrabi, radishes, small greens and lettuce. Use half-found containers made for attaching to a wall or fence. Make use of any space you find on a wall.

You can make a vertical wall using felt pouches, a modular tray or even planting tubes. Self-watering vertical living walls made from modular tray systems would be very productive. Numerous aeroponic garden systems are available to help you grow your vegetables vertically.

A tower garden planting system is a purchased vertical garden that can be used on any sunny place outside. A tower garden uses less than 10 percent of the water and land required by traditional soil-based gardens.

Chapter 43

BEST PLANTS FOR
HOMESTEADING

You don't have to live in a farm area to enjoy the fruits of your labor. Those living in suburbs and cities are learning how to live a lifestyle of self-sufficiency (homesteading) without ever leaving their comfortable homes in the city. As an example, you can grow up to 3 tons of organic produce annually on a 4000 square foot lawn.

You can grow vegetables without gardening skills. All it takes is a container to grow them in and a sunny spot to let them grow. Choose these five extremely easy vegetables to grow. Cut your grocery bill substantially, eat healthier and be self-sufficient.

- Lettuce grows fast and easy with very little organic soil and filtered water. You can grow lettuce indoors and in any container. Harvest your lettuce greens when they are young and enjoy the tender, fresh taste. Arugula and butter lettuce are high in nutrients and grow easily in small spaces. This same principle applies to spinach, kale, and other greens.

- Green beans are easy to grow. Bush beans are proliferate, and broad beans grow so easily that you will wonder why you did not consider growing them in the past. You will need to plant your beans with a trellis so they can climb.

- Carrots are the perfect root vegetable. You can plant carrot tops from organically grown products in soil and soon you will have new carrots. If you are planting, indoors make sure you have a deep pot. If you grow carrots in the ground and your soil is rocky, carrots will be crooked but will still be delicious. Take your ugly deformed carrots and make baby carrots out of them.

- Cucumbers grow with very little effort, and you can store them for years by pickling them. Cucumbers need a little extra space to grow, so they are not the best container vegetable. If you have a small plot of land, place them in the soil and watch them grow. Plant after the last hard frost. Cucumbers have fifteen health benefits and are a great addition to your self-sufficient lifestyle.

- Tomatoes grow well in containers and are best planted in the summer months. Tomatoes are a great starter plant for self-sufficient living. You can get starter plants from a nursery, or even start them from seed. Choose heirloom and organic varieties, so you can save seeds for growing future crops. Tomatoes do need lots of sun and must be watered well. A single tomato plant will produce all summer long.

- Growing ginger is not difficult. Plant this root vegetable in a pot and forget about it. Just water once in a while and these odd shaped plant roots will help prevent and reverse cancer, increase anti-inflammatory properties and boost your digestive health.

- Sweet potatoes are high in potassium, vitamins K and A, plus manganese, tryptophan, and beta carotene. These plants can be started from an old potato that has started to sprout. Cut off the eye that is growing and plant it in a pot with moist organic soil or in a garden spot. Sweet potatoes store well and will provide you with healthy food from many months.

- Onions are healthy foods that should be considered as part of your homestead garden. Onions are known to fight colon cancer, and have one of the highest levels of polyphenols.

- Grow garlic to spice up you meals and use as a blood cleanser, antibacterial, and antioxidant food. It boost the immune system and controls psoriasis, keep mosquitos and vampire away and treat athlete's foot. It is a great natural pesticide for plants.

- Choose the location of your square foot garden in a spot that gets at least six to eight hours of sun. Further scout out the location and plant your garden in an area where the morning sun hits the garden. Morning sun is much better for growing than afternoon sun, and a southeast exposure is optimal. You may want to plant your garden close to the house for ease of watering, weeding, and harvesting. However, because you are actually growing a small garden, it can be placed just about anywhere.

WHEN TO START YOUR GARDEN

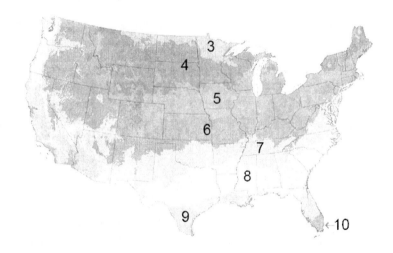

When to start your garden depends on where you live. In the Southeast you can garden for at least three seasons, but in the north you have a much smaller window of growing time.

Zone Map Key	
3	7
4	8
5	9
6	10

www.burpee.com

- This map of the United States give you growing zone information. Plant hardiness zones are based on average lowest winter temperatures. This is a good way to tell when to start planting and how long the growing season lasts.

- Zone 3's lowest winter temperatures are -40 to -30°F. Zone 4 is from -30 to -20°F, and if you are in Zone 5 watch for low temperatures of -20 to -10°F. In these zones you may want to start your garden between mid-May and mid-June. Check the hardiness of the plants you want to grow by reading the back of seed packets or the tags on plants starts.

- Zone 6's lowest temperatures are from -10 to 0°F, Zone 7 is from 0–10°, and Zone 8 is from 10 to 20°F. You can start crops in early to late April in these zones. If you live in Zone 6, however, you may want to start mid-May or after Mother's Day.

- If you are lucky enough to live in more temperate climates, Zone 9 is from 20–30°F and Zone 10's lowest temperatures range from 30 to 40°F.

Chapter 45

LAYOUT OF YOUR CROPS

Traditionally vegetable garden are in the form of plots of rows that are in large open backyards. Vegetable gardens are getting more and more popular, and urban gardening is trending. Large plots require quite a bit of attention and are not as prolific as some other types of gardening.

Small raised urban garden (www.vegetable-gardening-online.com)

Crop layouts should fit your lifestyle and accommodate those who have limited room for a traditional garden. Plant gardens in smaller beds. These save on space and allow the plants to grow closer together and provide the soil with shade and more moisture for crops.

Keep your crops in beds about 3 or 4 feet in width for easy maintenance. Divide beds with pathways to lessen the chances of having destroying crops by trampling on the plants. Add mulch and plastic or garden sheeting over the paths in your garden to keep weeds out and improve the appearance.

Plant early crops in such a way that you can plants other crops to take over. When earlier crops like peas are giving up, plant later crops in between the pea plants. This technique will keep your garden alive with continual growth.

Balcony vegetable garden (www.vegetable-gardening-online.com)

Plant taller plants like corn towards the back of your beds. You may also want to place the in the center with others crops working downward and to the sides.

Plant tomatoes, cucumbers and lettuce together. You now have a salad garden. Plant your root crops together. These crops include potatoes, sweet potatoes, carrots, and onions.

Chapter 46

WEEDS AND PESTS

Every gardener is challenged by insects, pests, and plant disease problems. Organic gardeners beg you to resist the urge to reach for an arsenal of chemical weapons. Chemical pesticides and herbicides may provide relief for the short term, but these chemical will also kill beneficial organisms. If you expose the environment to toxic organisms, you risk disrupting the ecosystem in your garden. Organic methods are much safer, more effective, and healthier.

Good Garden Insect - the Ladybug (www.
gardeninginfozone.com)

Organic pest control does not mean getting rid of all the insects. The vast majority or about 95% of insects in your garden are benign or beneficial. The organic approach requires you spend more time in your garden and take better care of your plants. Watch for early signs of insect attack or diseases.

Insects are important in the garden. There are insects that are pollinators, some break down organic matter, and there are insects that are beneficial predators finding their food in garden enemies. Identify your friends and foes. Use physical barriers, traps, and biological agents to assist in protecting your garden and helping maintain a healthy environment.

If your plants are stressed or unhealthy, they will be attacked. Grow your plants in healthy soil and add organic matter to your garden every year. Healthy soils provide the nutrient levels, soil structures, and water-holding capacity. Give your plants enough water and nutrients and supplement with organic fertilizers when necessary. Control weeds with mulches and use landscape fabric or plastic. Pull a few weeds every time you visit your garden. Thin seedlings so they are not overcrowded and give them good air circulation.

Rotate your crops to keep soil nutrients in balance. Your first year's crop of heavy feeders like tomatoes and lettuce can be followed up the next year by legumes or peas and beans. The third year you might let the soil "rest" by planting carrots or beets.

Keep your garden diverse. Plant smaller group of plants throughout the garden rather than planting all of your root crops in one place. Interplant herbs and flowers to protect you garden. Marigolds and nasturtiums repel insects. Dill, mint, and fennel attract those good insects that eat garden pests. Mixing pest repelling plants will give your vegetable garden a natural, healthy ecosystem.

Plant to avoid infestations (aufarief.wordpress.com)

Try scheduling your planting to avoid the heaviest feed stages of insects. Get familiar with patterns in your region. Talk to a greenhouse expert; they will know when and how to plant to avoid insect infestations.

Chapter 47

MAKING YOUR OWN FOOD

Making your own cheese can assure you of a fresh and healthy product without any added preservatives. Use fresh, raw milk from your local dairy or a dairy farmer who sells raw milk. Herd sharing is an awesome way of keeping your raw milk clean and nutritious. You can own an interest in a small herd of grass-fed cows and enjoy the brown-eyed Guernsey's and Jerseys with their soft muzzles and peaceful demeanors.

Farm cheese (nourishedkitchen.com)

To make cheese from your milk, start slow until you are expert. Process about a half-gallon a week, then move up to one gallon, then to two gallon and eventually to four gallons. Every week skim the cream off two gallons of milk. Use the skimmed milk for simple homemade farm cheese.

Farm Cheese Balls (nouishingjoy.com)

Making cheese involves purchasing a starter culture and rennet, or you can make cheese with heat and lemon juice or vinegar. Acidy ingredients, like lemon or vinegar, cause cheese curds to separate from the whey. Homemade cheese isn't nearly as complex as aged cheeses. Yu will not have a "hard" and savory product, but you will have a product with a milky, sweet and mild taste and texture.

This cheese, a simple and easy farm-style cheese, is quick to make and is an outstanding way of using up excess milk. (Paneer, a classic Indian cheese, is made this same way). Use simple farm cheese for snacks, as a substitute for mozzarella, or in casseroles. You will find that children love this simple, homemade farm cheese.

Ingredients
1 gallon raw milk
1/2 cup white vinegar
2 teaspoons very fine sea salt
Instructions
Line a colander with a double layer of cheesecloth.
Pour the milk into a heavy-bottomed kettle, and bring it to a boil over medium heat. Stir it frequently to keep the milk from scorching. When milk comes to a boil, immediately reduce the heat to low, and stir in the vinegar. The milk should immediately separate into curds and whey. If it does not separate, add a bit more vinegar one tablespoon at a time until you see the milk solids coagulate into curds. The whey should be a greenish bluish color.

Pour the curds and whey into the lined colander. Rinse gently with cool water, and sprinkle the curds with salt. Tie up the cheesecloth. Squeeze it with your hand to remove, the whey. Let the cheesecloth hang over the sink for 1 to 2 hours. Open up the cheesecloth and chop the cheese coarsely. Homemade farmer's cheese can be stored for up to a week in the refrigerator.

Organic Eggs

Organic eggs comes from chickens basically raised on small or family farms. Here they eat natural and certified organic feed. The chickens are also allowed to run free within a "field" confine. Organic eggs provide proteins, omega-e, essential vitamins and minerals. There are still ongoing questions whether or free range or "organic" chickens provide a better nutritional egg than regular store bought eggs and caged chickens. Organic eggs are certainly not less expensive. In order to provide your family with organic eggs grown on your own land, you have to purchase the chickens, build a coop, buy feed, and keep your chickens safe.

Organic eggs (with feathers) (ramonafarmersmarket.ning.com

Still, an organic egg farm has a higher level of oversight than a conventional chicken farm. Organic chicken farmers must maintain an organic certification and be inspected annually.

If you get your eggs from your own chickens or from a small organic farm, you may have pasture raised eggs. The hens are moved to a different patch of land every day and the fence pasts are shifted. This allows the chickens to peck for a new crop of grass and insects in addition to their certified organic feed.

Cage free and organic chicken flocks are smaller which keeps the chance of contamination with diseases and pests lower. However you do need to keep mice and rats out of the henhouse or your flocks may become infected.

It is emotionally satisfying to have your own chickens and eggs, but you be the judge as to which type (grocery, organic, or pasture) raised chickens and eggs are the best value.

Making Bread

Yummy Homemade Bread (www.eatingwell.com)

Learning to make your own bread will give you a sense of satisfaction, a healthy food addition to your diet, and provide your house with a wonderful smell that can't be purchased anywhere. Try making simple breads that have crusts that are never hard on the outside, but soft and artisan looking on the inside. Homemade bread is free from preservatives, artificial colors, and other strange chemicals.

This recipe comes from naturalmommie.com, Amanda, who lives green and helps bring eco-friendly and organic products into lives without being too "far out."

– 3 cups lukewarm water
– 1 1/2 tablespoons granulated yeast
– 1/2 tablespoon salt
– 1 tablespoon sugar
– 6 1/2 cups flour, unsifted, unbleached, all-purpose
These are the pretty much the same steps as my pizza dough recipe (which is incredible – go check it out now!) with a few little tweaks.
1. Grab a BIG mixing bowl. Or big container. Or bucket. I use huge rubbermaid containers that are about the size of a large lasagna pan.
2. Warm the water slightly. It should feel just a little warmer than body temperature. Warm water will rise the dough to the right point for storage in about 2 hours.
3. Add the yeast to the water in your big bowl & whisk, then add in sugar and salt. Don't worry about getting it all to dissolve.

4. Mix in the flour all at once. Kneading is unnecessary. Mix with a wooden spoon. You're finished when everything is uniformly moist, without dry patches. It takes a few minutes.

5. Cover with lid (not sealed or it'll explode off the top) or saran wrap leaving a pea-sized hole in the top to allow for gas to escape. Forget about it and let it rise for 2 hours (or let it rise overnight if you're making it before bed).

6. Once 2 hours is up, with floured hands reach in and grab a handful of dough about the size of a large grapefruit (for smaller loaves. use twice the amount for a decent size) You can shape it if you want...I usually just glob the dough on the parchment paper so when it's baked it looks more rustic :)

7. Let it sit on counter for 30-40 minutes on top of a parchment paper covered baking sheet.

Dust top with flour and use a serrated knife to make a few long slits on top.

9. Place on middle rack in preheated 425 degree oven. On bottom rack slide in a pie plate (or something similar) with 1 cup of water. The steam from the water below helps to make your crust amazingly chewy and not rock hard.

10. Bake for about 25 minutes (or until light golden brown or knock on it to see if it sounds hallow) and you're done!

Before you bake your bread you could also sprinkle shredded cheese on top (or in the dough while mixing), basil, Italian spices, Parmesan cheese, oatmeal – whatever. The beauty of this recipe is that you can make it anything you want! And TRY not to slice your bread until it's completely cooled for best result.

Chapter 48

PRESERVING YOUR GARDEN FOODS

Canning your own produce (nolagreenroots.com)

Canning

Can your own produce for the satisfaction of storing your home-grown food for later use. Learn to preserve food in case you need to have a food storage or for better-tasting and more nutritious food. You can be confident that your canned foods are free of preservatives and colorants. It is very empowering to see beautiful jars of bright vegetables lined up on shelves.

Every vegetable and fruit has its own special canning process. If you need more information, do can contact your local farmers exchange or log onto CanningPantry.com, kerr.com, homecanning. com or any other canning website. Most have the same instructions. Do note that you will have to purchase glass jars, lids and rings and possibly a pressure canner. It is not inexpensive to start canning, but as time goes on you will have to purchase fewer supplies; just recycle from last year.

Dehydrating and Drying

Drying your produce is one of the oldest methods for preserving foods. Dried foods need less space than canned foods, and you can often eat dehydrated foods without reconstituting them.

Dehydrated food in airtight containers (modernsurvivalblog.com)

Drying vegetables means removing enough moisture from foods to prevent decay and spoilage. You will need to use enough heat to draw out moisture without cooking the food; have dry air to absorb the released moisture, and adequate air circulation to carry off the moisture.

Remove the moisture as quickly as possible at a temperature that does not affect the texture, color or flavor of the vegetables. You may have to use a trial and error approach to see what type of dehydrating and drying is best for your situation.

Drying trays need good air circulation. For small amounts of food, use cheesecloth stretched over oven racks, cake racks or cookie sheets. Do not use galvanized screening for tray bottoms. If your trays have been treated with zinc and cadmium, you will experience harmful reactions when these metals come in contact with acidy foods. Do not use aluminum; this metal corrodes.

Wash trays, preferably wooden, rinse, and air dry. Use fresh vegetable oil to coat the surface. Place blocks of wood at least two inches between trays.

Select vegetables at peak flavor and eating quality. Peak quality is just as they reach maturity. Dry sweet corn and green peas when they are slightly immature, so they keep the sweet flavor.

Yield of dried vegetables.

Beans, lima 7 1 1/4 2	Beans, snap 6 1/2 2 1/2	Beets 15 1 1/2 3 to 5
Broccoli 12 1 3/8 3 to 5	Carrots 15 1 1/4 2 to 4	Celery 12 3/4 3 1/2 to 4
Corn 18 2 1/2 4 to 4 1/2	Greens 3 1/4 5 1/2	Onions 12 1 1/2 4 1/2
Peas 8 3/4 1	Pumpkin 11 3/4 3 1/2	Squash 10 3/4 5
Tomatoes 14 1/2 2 1/2 to 3		

Source: Drying Foods at Home, Marjorie M. Philips, Cooperative

Steps for Drying Vegetables

Blanching Drying

Vegetable Preparation Time* (mins.) Time (hrs.) Dryness test

Asparagus Wash thoroughly. Halve large tips. 4-5 6-10 Leathery to brittle	Beans, green Wash. Cut in pieces or strips. 4 8-14 Very dry, brittle	Beets Cook as usual. Cool, peel. Cut into shoestring None 10-12 Brittle, dark red	Strips 1/8" thick.	Broccoli Wash. Trim, cut as for serving. Quarter stalks lengthwise. 4 12-15 Crisp, brittle
Brussels sprouts Wash. Cut in half lengthwise through stem. 5-6 12-18 Tough to brittle	Cabbage Wash. Remove outer leaves, quarter and core. Cut into strips 4 10-12 Crisp, brittle 1/8" thick.	Carrots, parsnips Use only crisp, tender vegetables. Wash. 4 6-10 Tough to brittle Cut off roots and tops; peel. Cut in slices or strips 1/8" thick.	Cauliflower Wash. Trim, cut into small pieces. 4-5 12-15 Tough to brittle	Celery Trim stalks. Wash stalks and leaves thoroughly. Slice stalks. 4 10-16 Very brittle

Chili peppers, green Wash. To loosen skins, cut slit in skin, then rotate over flame 6-8 None 12-24 Crisp, brittle,	Minutes or scald in boiling water. Peel and split pods. medium green	Remove seeds and stem. (Wear gloves if necessary.)	Chili peppers, red Wash thoroughly. Slice or leave whole if small. 4 12-24 Shrunken, dark red pods, flexible	Corn, cut Husk, trim. Wash well. Blanch until milk in corn is set. Cut 4-6 6-10 Crisp, brittle
kernels from the cob.	Eggplant Wash, trim, cut into 1/4" slices. 4 12-14 Leathery to brittle	Horseradish Wash, remove small rootlets and stubs. Peel or scrape roots. Grate. None 6-10 Brittle, powdery	Mushrooms** Scrub. Discard tough, woody stalks. Slice tender stalks 1/4" thick. None 8-12 Dry and leathery	Peel large mushrooms, slice. Leave small mushrooms whole. Dip in solution of 1 tsp. citric acid/ quart water 10 minutes. Drain.
Okra Wash thoroughly. Cut into 1/2" pieces or split lengthwise. 4 8-10 Tough, brittle	Onions Wash, remove outer paper skin. Remove tops and root ends, 4 6-10 Very brittle	slice 1/8 to 1/4" thick.	Parsley; other herbs Wash thoroughly. Separate clusters. Discard long or tough stems. 4 4-6 Flaky	Peas Shell and wash. 4 8-10 Hard, wrinkled,

green	Peppers; pimentos Wash, stem. Remove core and seeds. Cut into 1/4 to 1/2" 4 8-12 Tough to brittle	strips or rings.	Potatoes Wash, peel. Cut into 1/4" shoestring strips or 1/8" thick slices. 7 6-10 Brittle	Spinach; greens like Trim and wash very thoroughly. Shake or pat dry to remove 4 6-10 Crisp
Kale, Chard, mustard excess moisture.	Squash, summer Wash, trim, cut into 1/4" slices. 4 10-16 Leathery to brittleor banana	Squash, winter Wash rind. Cut into pieces. Remove seeds and cavity pulp. 4 10-16 Tough to brittle	Cut into 1" wide strips. Peel rind. Cut strips crosswise into pieces	about 1/8" thick.
Tomatoes Steam or dip in boiling water to loosen skins. Chill in cold water. None 6-24 Crisp	Peel. Slice 1/2" thick or cut in 3/4" sections. Dip in solution of 1 tsp. citric acid/ quart water for 10 minutes.	*Blanching times are for 3,000 to 5,000 feet. Times will be slightly shorter for lower altitudes and slightly longer for higher altitudes or for large quantities of vegetables.		

Freezing

Freezing your excess garden vegetables is fast and easy. You can freeze most crops like broccoli, green beans, peppers, summer squash, peas, and all type of berries. Corn is awesome when frozen fresh. You can freeze your vegetables in small batches or one big batch from your homegrown harvest. You don't have to pay attention to acidity or salt when freezing your vegetables. Just mix and match vegetables based on colors and flavors or your family's favorites.

Frozen herbs (www.keeperof thehome.org)

Add carrots, peas and corn for a great vegetable is that tastes awesome in the middle of the winter. Blanch mild onions and freeze so you don't have to chop onions when you need them for cooking. Avoid adding any seed spices to your vegetables; just freeze them in their natural state.

Freeze vegetables flat on cookie sheets. You can steam–blanch and freeze – hollowed out, stuffable squash, zucchini, eggplants, and peppers. You can even blanch and freeze cabbage leaves to use for cabbage rolls.

Use only fruits and vegetables that are in excellent condition and have been cleaned. Blanch them for two to five minutes. Blanching is the process of heating vegetables with boiling water for a small amount of time. You then immediately plunge boiled produce into cold or icy water. Cooled veggies can be packed into bags, jars or freezer safe storage containers.

Remove as much air as possible from the freezer containers. When using zip-close freezer bags, squeeze all the air out by hand.

Salt Preservation

Curing and preserving via salt is often used with meats, fish and some vegetables. You use a combination of salt, nitrates, nitrite and or sugar. You may also cure your meats by smoking. Salting draws moisture form the meats through a process of osmosis.

Salt is essential in the human diet. Your body cannot manufacture salt so you have to ingest salt to replace what is lost through sweat. Sodium chloride is about .28% of the human body weight. However, if you ingest too much salt you will experience serious health problems. The balance is very delicate, but the USDA recommends a daily sodium consumption of less than a teaspoon.

You can use pickling salt for a preservative, but plain old fashioned table salt is also affective.

Salt-Preserved Greens (Kale)
2 cups kale 2 tablespoons salt 1/3 cup rice or cider vinegar 1 large garlic clove, sliced 1/2 teaspoon ground ginger, optional 1/8 teaspoon red pepper flakes, optional
Carefully wash kale and de-rib. Roll leaves and finely slice into ribbons.
Place in glass jar. Mix remaining ingredients and pour over greens. Add warm water if needed to fill up jar. Stir gently. Refrigerate for at least 1 hour until chilled, or overnight. To serve, drain and rinse. Toss with a little vegetable oil and lemon juice. To garnish, sprinkle sesame seeds on top.

Preserve meats with salt. This method was used as far back as history records. Salt has a preservative effect due to the osmotic pressure it crease as it is absorbed. Preserving meat with salt is simple and straightforward. There are a variety of variations on the basic method, but the instructions are generally accepted. Rinse the fresh meat in cold water then pour a thin layer of sale (generally kosher salt) all over the meat and rub it in. Hang or set the meat out in a cool room that is under 60 degrees Fahrenheit, but not below freezing. Allow it to hang for a couple of weeks to dry out.

Salt preserved deer meat (www.pinterest.com)

It is claimed that if you use enough salt when drying meat you can preserve meat for a very long time. If you are only preserving meat for a short time, it is generally considered that a 20% salt concentration on the surface of the meat is all that is needed to kill off microbes and fungi that spoil meats quickly.

Chapter 49

URBAN HOMESTEADING

www..urbanghostsmedia.com

Urban Homesteading is using heirloom skills for sustainable living. This homesteading movement is spreading across the nation and those who want to reduce their impact on the environment are turning to growing and preserving their own foods. Learn ecology in the city. Provide for your basic needs close to where you live. Self-reliance that comes from your own ground rather than the grocery store will give you great satisfaction, health, and a new lease on life.

Chapter 50

VERTICAL GARDENING

Vertical gardens are the trendiest movement in gardening for homeowners, commercial and office buildings, hospitals, restaurants or just about any business concerned with the environment. Vertical gardens are perfect solutions for any space – indoors or out–that cries out for creativity. Vertical garden elements draw attention to an area you want to emphasize or disguise an unattractive view.

Have you ever noticed that plants just make you feel better? It is a scientific fact that plants and green walls lower your blood pressure, improve your reaction times, and increase attentiveness. (Notice how attentive, happy and relaxed you are the next time you walk through a green space or park.)

Living green walls improve air quality inside as well as outside. They filter air pollution, take away unsavory smells and improve your personal environment with the intrinsic benefits of nature. Plant a green wall and just create a "wow" factor.

If you are an apartment dweller or a small space urban gardener, vertical gardening is perfect for you. Those who are disabled and cannot bend to weed and harvest traditional gardens, a vertical garden may be the answer. Vertical gardens can be combined with container gardens to produce even more vegetables and flowers and artistic spaces. If you want a vegetable garden, but you think your apartment, physical disability, or small yard prohibits a garden, you are very wrong. You can always try container gardening that is awesome, but it does take up valuable space. Vertical gardening will give you an entirely new perspective on growing fruits, vegetables, flower or other splendid plants.

Don't just limit yourself to outside vertical gardening. Think outside the exterior vertical garden and go indoors. Indoors you can grow small houseplants and make a living wall. Surround your favorite plants in a unique frame, or add plants to a trellis inside the front door. Indoor plants are cheerful and really do filter out air pollutants. Not to mention the other health benefits of a stress free environment, ambiance, and just plain happy feelings.

Green or living walls are considered vertical gardening. You may have an outside wall covered with climbing plants; that's a vertical garden. If you have hanging plants, you have a vertical garden. Design a more formal structure that allows unusual plants to grow up walls. The trend is to grow succulents in frames and on walls. Your imagination is only limited by the number of walls you have or the vertical space you can invent.

Vertical gardening in coffee cans hung on
a wall (www.socialmoms.com)

Include in your vertical gardening system spaces for soilless potting mediums so you can add many different types of plants. You may also need an irrigation system. Note that green walls require pruning, dusting, weeding and at times you will need to replace a plant or two. Due to the soil, plants, and watering, vertical gardening system walls are heavy. Study and build your structure to hold the soil and plants you choose for your garden.

Vertical gardens are spot-on for:

- Maximizing limited space.

- Creating a garden room. Using vertical structures like arches, pergolas, arbors and gazebos, you can create ambiance in your outdoor garden. Add small garden tables and chairs, and you have created an outdoor living space.

- Disguise unwanted views and unattractive outside structures by growing a vertical privacy screen.

- Plants are easier to reach and take care of if they are grown vertically. Plus, you won't have a sore back and aching knees after taking care of your standing garden.

- Plants are healthier if they are grown off the ground. Airflow improves, there are less pests and disease problems, and your pet can't dig up your precious vegetables and flowers.

- You can grow more plants vertically. Train your pumpkins to grow up and over a trellis or an unsightly fence.

- Vertical gardening reduces the impact of an urban environment. You can soften stark building walls and landscape surfaces by camouflaging them with green walls.

Vertical gardening in soda bottles. (mofur.blogspot.com)

Improve the air quality and thus your health. Research proves that plants improve indoor and outdoor air quality. They remove harmful volatile organic compounds and absorb pollutants. Grow plants vertically in your home on windowsills, in front entrances and hang those plants around every room.

Chapter 51

WHAT TO CONSIDER WHEN GROWING A VERTICAL GARDEN

Vertical garden designers are exploring different mediums and places to grow plants. Thoughts are turning to vertical gardening with almost endless ways to bring the outdoors inside. Your vegetable plants produce more crops by growing vertical. Vines and flowers love to stand upright. Every plant benefits from standing up and being vertical. However, before you start adding shelves and wall containers to the empty spaces on the wall in and outside your home, consider these five factors.

- Sunlight. Plants make their own food by using sunlight and breaking it down through photosynthesis. They inhale CO_2 and release fresh oxygen. A vertical garden requires at least four to six hours of sunlight each day. Place your vertical garden on a southern wall, inside and outside, to get vital amounts of sunlight.

- Water. Plants cannot grow without water. Water starts the germination process and activates enzymes in seeds that encourage growth. Keep your vertical garden near a hose or water faucet or purchase a vertical gardening wall that has a watering system of its own. Install a drip system on a timer to keep a vertical garden watered and not drowned.

Recycled bottles showcase a fresh vertical vegetable garden www.finecraftguild.com

Be environmental and reuse containers. You can use just about anything to plant vertically. Hang containers on walls, use hanging baskets, and investigate companies who make environmentally safe pucks and inserts for walls. Built your own vertical system by using recycled materials and your own ingenuity.

- Be patient. Vertical gardening is exciting, and it does show that you are eco-minded. However, vertical gardening is maintenance intensive. You need to keep your garden bug and weed free just like it's on the ground. Plant natural plant flower pesticides like marigolds that give you a visual benefit, as well as a practicality. Prune, when needed and do, keep out the weeds.

- Root depth. Consider how deep plants need to shoot their roots. Carrots and beets require a foot and a half of a soil while lettuce requires only a few inches. There are some crops that are designed to stay in the ground like potatoes. Don't just plant anything you want, think about the different plants and how heavy they can be.

Training your vegetables to grow vertically provide may benefits. These include:

- Space saving. Grow and harvest vegetables in spaces that you would not think could be a garden.

- Vertical gardening makes vegetables easier to harvest.

- You are providing your garden with better air circulation. Better air circulation provides healthy conditions for growing plants.

- Vegetables stay off the ground and mold, soil borne diseases, crawling insects or other pests cannot reach fruits or leaves as quickly as they attack ground plants.

Chapter 52

Structures for Vertical Gardens

You can use wooden or metal trellises, shelves, containers, hanging baskets, a wood frame or just about any combination of these structures to create a space-saving vertical garden. Do double duty and utilize space by growing both upwards and on the ground.

Easy does it vertical garden trellis. forums.gardenweb.com

Trellises are perfect for support trailing vine crops. Use a fence as a trellis for beans, peas, tomatoes and squash and cucumbers. Take advantage of vertical space and use corn stalks or sunflowers as supports for beans and climbing vegetables. Stepladders are marvelous for supporting vine-growing plants like pumpkins. Train the vines to go up and down the ladder and place the vegetables on the steps. Step ladders also work as shelves to house tomato plants, interspersed with marigolds, cucumbers, and small squash.

Consider your front porch. Your vertical garden can climb up the posts that hold up the roof over your front porch. If you are renting and need something portable, use structures that are lightweight and can be easily moved. An unattached vertical trellis filled with hanging pots is a wonderful way to create a garden.

Position hanging baskets and planters where you won't hit them as you walk past. Make sure there is adequate support for the weight of mature fruits and water in the hanging basket. Try not to hang your vertical garden too high or it will be difficult to maintain.

Select a structure that will hold the weight of mature plants. You might want to avoid vertically growing heavy plants like melons and pumpkins across a rickety fence or on a lightweight frame.

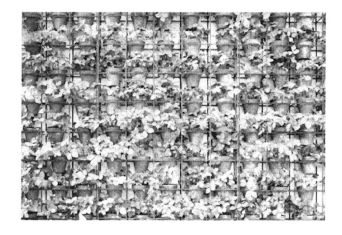

Vertical Garden on an outside wall. (gardenista.com)

Just get creative. You will find something that works for you and your situation by wandering through greenhouses and gardening shops. Have a bountiful harvest of freshly grown vegetables without taking up space.

If you have a wall that's ugly, that's the wall to decorate with a vertical garden. Almost any old wall will do, just follow the rules of staking, supporting, and sunning.

1Hydroponic garden tower (diply.cm - Pinterest)

Shelves are awesome for vertical vegetable and flower gardening. Any of the space "hogs" in your vegetable garden can easily be trained to grow up instead of out. Growing up and using shelves takes only one-tenth of the space of a traditional garden. Think about adding container gardening to a shelving systems. Plants that don't climb like lettuce, peppers, radishes, onions, eggplants and all types of herbs love to be up and away from the rest of the garden. This way they can get all the air and nutrients they need.

Start by building a frame. The basic structure of a vertical wall is a three-layer unit with a frame plastic sheeting and fabric.

Chapter 53

BUILDING A VERTICAL GARDEN

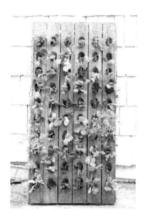

Vertical Garden Wall off a Deck. www.123rf.com

Vertical Garden in Wood (homes-kid.com)

Your vertical garden structure can be a purchased arbor, pergola, trellis, or make your own. A pergola is also known as an arbor and is an area of vertical posts that support cross-beams and open lattice. Vines are gorgeous when trailing up and down and across the roof of a pergola.

A trellis is a structure made in an open framework design that is made to support and display climbing plants. Trellises can be a viticulture or covered with vines and used for grapes, clematis, ivy and climbing roses. Metal trellises are ornate, and they are not the best choice for climbing plants. The sun will heat the metal and stunt the growth of many vines.

Garden vertically outdoors, but take into consideration several different factors. You will need to anchor your vertical garden structure before planting. Anchoring allows you to avoid disturbing the roots. If you have heavy or demanding plants, place them on heavier structures.

Vertical gardens cast shadows, and this can affect the growing patterns of ground plants. Place your garden structures in areas where they will not shade ground plants.

Be aware that plants grow differently on a vertical garden. Climbing roses must be physically attached to structures, but other flower types like morning glories will loop themselves around trellis openings.

Vertical gardens need more watering and fertilizing since vertically grown plants are exposed to greater amounts of sun and wind.

Begin your vertical garden by using an iron frame, garden rack or heavy duty trellis. Or, build a do-it-yourself (DIY) vertical garden can be built using these materials:

Beginning of a vertial wall garden (stephanielynn.com)

4-6 pieces of 10x5zx5 cm to hold the garden rack from the wall

Planks or slats to line the frame

Plastic sheeting

Jute cloth to hold the earth to the frame. Make this the size of your garden rack, plus about 20 cm on the long sides

Dowel, screws and cramp-irons plus small connecting strips or corners

A drill

Hammer

Screwdriver

Saw

1. Paint or use a protectant on the wood to keep the wood from decaying.

2. Line up the planks, they will be used to line the frame and make it solid. You will need to have a solid frame to hold the weight of the soil you use. Saw the planks to the size of your frame. You should have three piece: a short one that goes at the top of the frame, and two long planks for the sides.

3. Wooden blocks that are 10x5x5 cm are used to attach the frame to the wall. Drill a hole through the wooden blocks and screw the wood to the supporting wall.

Lay the frame on the ground and attach the three planks to the frame. Use iron cramps. Turn the frame over and attach planks at the top using connecting strips.

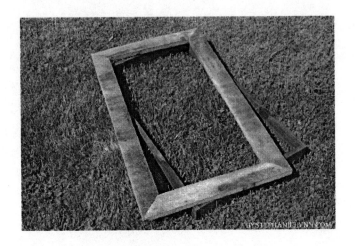

Line the planter with landscape fabric (Stephanielyn.com)

Place a piece of plastic sheeting the wall behind the frame. Plastic sheeting will keep moisture and humidity away from the wall.

1. Attach the frame to the wall at four points. These points are the top right and left corners and near the mid-point of the structure on both sides. Secure the bottom of the frame.

2. The trickiest part of your vertical garden is attaching the jute cloth to the wall. This is where the wooden blocks come into play. These blocks need to be on the inside of the cloth when finished. Take one of the wood blocks and the jute. Put a screw in the corner of the jute and screw it into the hole you made in the block. Do the same with the remaining three blocks.

3. Now, place a screw through the planks where the wood blocks are, and use this screw to attach the frame to the wood blocks.

4. Cut away the excess plastic sheet around your vertical garden. You are nearing the end!

5. Mix in plenty of compost with your soil. Begin by filling the frame with compost and soil. Fill up the garden about halfway up the wall and water it down. Finish filling the wall with dirt and water down.

6. Plant hardy, but small plants. Plant some perennials to keep the earth alive over the winter. Vines, tomato plants, beans, squash, and flowers will grow wonderfully on this wall. Poke a hole in the jute to hold the roots of the plants. Keep well hydrated, fertilized (natural, of course), and enjoy your growing wall.

7. If this design sounds too complicated, try using ¾ inch PVC pipe, elbows and four wall joints to build a frame. Do not use metal, it is expensive, too heavy and get too hot. Wood is great, as in the previous illustration but PVC pipe is lighter, resistance to heat and weather, and looks great.

Attach plastic sheeting to the frame. The plastic is a backing for the fabric layer and to keep water off the wall. Attach the layer of fabric to the frame. This is the material where your plants will happily live and the medium to hold water. You can use basic felt carpet padding or any fabric that will retain water and not rot. Add two layers of fabric. Attach the fabric directly to the frame and use galvanized screws and stainless steel staples. Keep the fabric taut with no wrinkles and you are ready to plant. Make sure it is attached so it won't come off. Fabric backing also adds dimension to your living art piece.

You will need an irrigation system that provides moisture throughout the fabric layers. The irrigation system can be basically a tube system run across the top of your panel with holes to let water drip (not pour) down. You can find these types of pipes at an irrigation supply store.

Add fertilizer to your water system to keep nutrients constantly moving throughout your wall. There will always be some runoff. Plant a flower bed underneath your vertical garden.

If you are handy but don't have the time to build your own vertical gardening wall, there are vertical garden planters you can get at your local garden stores. These vertical garden planters are usually made from recycled PET plastic and felt and are mounted on a rigid plastic panel or frame. You simply hang your vertical garden structure to the wall with provided nylon tabs, line the pockets with dirt, plant your plants and watch them grow. Some commercial vertical walls include drip lines for ease of watering.

Chapter 54

VERTICAL GARDEN CONTAINERS

Trellis (media.feeneyinc.com)

Simple vertical garden against a wooden fence. (www.bhg.com)

Think of your hanging baskets as a vertical garden. Hanging baskets can be classified as vertical gardening containers because they break up the horizontal plane of a wall, space or garden. Any structure that draws the eyes up from the ground like a trellis, obelisks, or a wall can be used as a vertical gardening space. Hanging baskets fit this definition and create more garden space, give you more color and room to grow food. If you are an urban gardener with little space, plant predominately in containers, take advantage of hanging baskets. This will be the beginning to your vertical wall garden.

You can grow vegetables virtually anywhere. Use wooden crates, gallon sized cans, old washtubs and just about anything that you can add dirt. Add these interesting containers to shelves. Shelves are awesome to use as a growing area. You can grow numerous types of vegetables on each shelf and position the vertical vegetable garden so all the plants receive adequate amounts of sunlight. Use shelving that is made with slats. Slats allow better air circulation and water can drip down to the plants below. You can add containers on shelves or place them in tiers. Tiering your garden gives your vertical garden an awesome appearance.

England Trellis (tellisstruture.com)

Think outside the garden for containers. You can use anything that can be hung on a wall or set on a shelf. One of the most unique vertical garden containers is a shoe bag. Put dirt and plants in the pocket and hang it on your back door, or a fence or even on a tree. You can plant flowers, vegetables, or vines in a shoe hanging bag.

Once the plants grow, no one will know what the container really is. Wht an awesome conversation starter!

Garden trellis are traditional. They are essentially garden posts that grow upwards and the watering duties are easy to manage. You can do a lean too trellis against a garage wall or put an Eiffel Tower trellis right in the middle of your garden. Elevated planter boxes are types of vertical gardening and make space for pants to be grown underneath. A simple expandable pea trellis will be perfect for those spring peas that love to grow towards the sun.

Plants for Hanging Baskets

Food and flowers in a vertical garden (hanging basket.) Photo: Chris McLaughlin

Lettuce thrives in baskets. Create your own salad by planting several lettuce varieties, add some herbs and flowers into your hanging basket. Personality plus color and lunch. You can plant young vegetables and flowers by poking holes in the sides and planting them. As they grow, the effect will be stunning.

Grow eggplants, strawberries, peppers, cherry tomatoes and mustard greens in your hanging basket. Herbs are naturals in hanging baskets. Keep your hanging baskets watered, fertilized and give your plants a break in the shade once in a while.

Be creative with what you plant. One hanging basket that was the hit last spring was a mix of cucumbers, cilantro, and hot peppers. Cherry tomatoes were added as the base of the salsa hanging basket.

You have seen those gorgeous flower hanging baskets just about everywhere. You purchase a commercial hanging basket, take it home and it dies within a few weeks. You are out the money and the emotion. Try making your own. Choose plants that are long trailing plants like trailing petunias. These are planted on the top of your basket, Purple verbena can be planted on the sides of the basket as well as the top to fill out your basket. Pick plants that are healthy with several stems. Choose plants in 2 ½ inch containers. This size of plant is very easy to insert through wire frames.

Peat based soil mixes are used for hanging baskets, but you need to add some loam-or human based potting soils. Give your plants a good helping of kelp meal. Monitor moisture levels in vertical baskets. Water thoroughly, but allow your basket to dry out slightly between waterings. Fertilize with iron every other watering, and use slow release beads.

Build and Plant a Hanging Basket

- Wire-frame basket that is16 inches across and 9 to 11 inches deep.

- Wood-fiber liner; cut to fit the frame.

- 8-inch plastic water saucer

- 51 inches of 1/2-inch vinyl tubing

- 16 quarts of hanging-basket soil (lightweight) plus 4 quarts of humus-based potting soil), and one tablespoon kelp meal.

- 4 quarts of water

- One tablespoon slow-release, 15-15-15 fertilizer beads

Gorgeous Hanging Planter. (www.bhg.com)

Plants in 2-1/2-inch pots. Use 15 short-trailing plants, or six trailing petunias such as

Hang from a wall or post: a sturdy bracket with a horizontal bar. If you want a bushy balled effect chose a variety of annuals. Make sure you have a trailing plants. Plant taller varieties in the center, and trailing or vining plants around the edges.

- Hang overhead using a 1-1/2-inch screw hook, an S hook, and a length of chain.

Grow this strawberry hanging basket right and have
fruit all season (www.gardenersworld.com)

Fruits and vegetables can also been grown in a hanging, vertical garden.

Just make your container to have excellent drainage, a stout hanging chain, and nutrient rich and clean soil. Keep the moisture constant and protect from strong winds. Use cherry tomatoes or strawberries and the vining portion of your vertical hanging planter. Stake taller vegetables in the middle and plant lettuce around the edges. Do feed well. Hanging vegetable plants do very well with liquid fertilizer applied at least once per week at watering time.

Chapter 55

PLANTS FOR VERTICAL GARDENING

Experiment with plant options, but do consider light and shade. You have many choices, and there are plant choices you may not have considered. Take a chance and do something adventurous. You can always change your mind and adjust your plantings to suit the habitat. Create a custom living wall based on your awesome creativity. It is wonderful to experiment with colors, textures, vines, vegetables and fruits. Let your vertical garden become your natural art piece.

Go crazy with vertical gardening. You can have a gorgeous yard with fruits and vegetables and flowers on the walls around the outside of our home. Use vines in your vertical garden. Vines grow down or up, but always vertically. Some vines attach by using tendrils that climb, twine, and cling. Be careful that you have a frame for your vine vertical garden. Vines that climb using tendrils will dig into wall materials and cause damage to the building.

Vegetables

Tomatoes growing vertically. (buchanansplants.com)

There are many awesome varieties of vegetables that can be used in your vertical garden. Cherry tomatoes, snap peas, pole beans, plus cucumbers, and some types of the lighter squashes are perfect. These are plants that work their runners up the fence, box or trellis. Just give them directions. If you stake your tomatoes, you are already a vertical gardener. Your plants are producing fruit all along the stem and they are climbing to the sun.

Fruits

Fruits like grapes and berries are common in vertical gardens. You can also grow small melons that can be support by a heavier vertical framework.

Flowers

Flowering plant used in vertical plants include morning glory, nasturtium, climbing roses and jasmine. Some gardeners use wisteria and sweet peas to complete their vertical gardening look. Vertical gardens full of flowers attract birds and butterflies. You can grow flowering vine plants on a trellis or directly on a building.

Just about any type of vine flower can be grown vertically. Take advantage of what nature has to offer and build your own green garden wall.

Vines and Climbers

Vertical vine production (badgr.uvm.edu)

Small vines are perfect for vertical gardening. They easily climb a trellis or structure without growing out of their space. Top picks for vines include the Tasmanian blueberry vine. It is a very tough and hardy vine that grows to about 10 feet tall.

Chilean bellflower booms nonstop and has a tropical looking hanging bell shaped flower. Usually this vine is vivid red and does not grow all over the place.

White evergreen clematis is the smallest of the clematis family and has very glossy green leaves. It is only four feet tall and is easy to train to grow up an obelisk or a trellis.

Ivy is perfect for vertical gardening. English ivy is spot-on, but you can use Boston ivy, honeysuckle, Virginia creepers and trumpet vines. These are examples of different ivy. Do be aware that these vines can become invasive if you leave them unchecked and they do need weeding, pruning and watering.

Some plants are natural twiners, but others need to be tied to a support. Use trellises, pergolas, arbors, poles, lattice, stakes, tee pees, cages or fences for vine support. Use garden twine to prevent bruising or cutting into the stems. Never use metal to tie your vies to a support.

Chapter 56

INDOOR VERTICAL GARDENING

G rowing a living wall is just like growing plants in containers. You have seen these vertical garden walls in the courtyards of office buildings, so why not create a green space in your own home?

Green wall added to a rock wall to create a stunning living environment. (www.homes-kid.com)

Plants are scientifically proven to improve air quality. Have you ever heard the phrase, "the Amazon rainforest is the lungs of the world?" Green walls will improve the quality of the air in any environment. It is a natural air filter and purifies polluted air. Think about a green wall in an office environment. Green walls lead to greater employee productivity and overall health. In your home, a green wall will add design punch and improve your overall health.

Esthetics are improved with a living wall. Imagine your guests walking into your home and seeing a living wall. Green walls are awesome for creating good first impressions in a business. Be unique, plant a vertical garden wall.

Installing a green wall in your home acts as a natural air conditioner. Green walls balance humidity levels and keep the air comfortable. Though evapotranspiration the air surrounding a living wall is naturally cooler.

Did you known that a grouping of plants reduces noise levels. A living wall will decrease background noise in communal dining areas or reduce noise pollution from the neighbors. Foliage absorbs and reflects noise. If there is a room in your home you want to turn into a peaceful haven, try vertical gardening indoors.

Garden wall in home in Camden, London. (www.the-guardian.com – photographer – Sophia Evans)

Gutters from the junkyard. (Shutterstock)

You can install a vertical garden space inside your home by yourself. Select the space you want to use for your green wall. Build a frame and make sure it is solid and can be hung or leaned on a wall. Attach plastic sheeting to the frame to prevent water from leaking all over the floor.

Attach a layer of fabric, felt works best, which acts as the foundation where your plants will grow. Set up an irrigation system for water. You can attach a tube across the top of your wall, and water will drip down throughout the entire structure. Consult an expert at this point.

There are many different ways you can develop a living wall. Use recycled materials. A picture frame is easy and would be awesome. Start with an old frame, attach chicken wire to the frame. Hold the wire in place with a second frame. Fill with soil, plant and water.

Choose and insert the plants you want in your green wall. What plant you choose is personal preference. Take into account the room and what you want the room to "say." An herb garden in a kitchen would be perfect or make a vertical garden wall of vegetables. Plant a selection of flowering greenery and vines. Use succulents to make a living wall. Be careful, however that you choose plants that are easy care and don't need direct sunlight.

The only difference between an outdoor and indoor vertical garden wall is the size and weight. Indoor vertical gardens tend to be smaller and not so heavy. Be aware that your indoor vertical wall garden can be messy if you use the wrong materials. Check with a local design company; they know the tips and tricks of indoor garden walls.

Chapter 57

QUICK OVERVIEW

Why would you grow a vertical garden? First and foremost is space. It is more efficient to grow up rather than on the ground. If you are growing squash, zucchini or cucumbers don't let these plants take over your garden, grow them vertically and take them off the ground.

If you have limited sunlight, maximize what light have. Growing vertically in sunny spots allows you to maximize light. This saves the ground for more-shade tolerant crops.

There are many different type of plants you can grow vertically. Think about beans, peas and scarlet runner bans. Think outside the box and plant vertically challenged vegetables. How about growing Baby Bear pumpkins vertically or trellising black berries. What about those huge tomato vines. They will grow vertically if you attach them to a trellis or garden wall system.

Don't let the traditional stop you from using vining vegetables to cover an unattractive fens or sneaking lettuce into your hanging baskets. Use an old shoe bag as a wall planter for small plants and create a trellis for your sidewalk and cover it with vegetable plants.

Use a trellis, either DIY or purchased to convince your plants to grow up rather than crawling on the ground. Keep an eye, literally, on those pests. You will see them as they climb up your vegetables and you can better control them.

Harvesting is so much easier with a vertical garden. There is no more stooping or hunching over. You won't waste as much overripe fruits since nothing is hidden in bushy growths.

Build your trellises along the north side of your garden and anchor your trellises to protect them from wind and plant weights. Sink them at least 24 inches deep.

Be adventurous when planting vertically. Grow tomatoes, peas and cucumbers, pole beans and gourds and melons. You can also grow miniature pumpkins and acorn and butternut squash. It is so exciting just to anticipate what can be grown vertically and to get ready to build that trellis, or wall, or fun planters.

Involve your entire family in vertical gardening. Start small and don't get overwhelmed and allow children to help plants seeds and plants and watch them grow from their level.

Use your vertical gardening containers and habits to add attraction to your ground garden. Use several trellises in your garden. Fill them with vegetables, fruits, and lush vines. Don't go out and spend a crazy amount of money to assemble your vertical garden. The coolest vertical gardening systems are put together with found and re-cycled materials. Up-cycled old wooden pallets, bottles, cans and gutters off your house. Lash bamboo poles together for vegetables to climb on and create trellises from string and wooden frames. Just be creative. You will be amazed at what you have all around you that will support a vertical garden.

Pallets and Plants (Shutterstock)

WAIT! – DO YOU LIKE
FREE BOOKS?

My **FREE Gift** to You!! As a way to say **Thank You** for downloading my book, I'd like to offer you more **FREE BOOKS!** Each time we release a NEW book, we offer it first to a small number of people as a test - drive. Because of your commitment here in downloading my book, I'd love for you to be a part of this group. You can join easily here → **http://gardening-mastery.com/**

CHECK OUT THESE #1 BEST SELLING

BOOKS FROM JOY LOUIS!

http://www.amazon.com/Joy-Louis/e/B00UMOZJE6

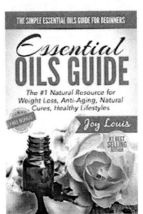

Conclusion

Thank you again for downloading this book!

If you enjoyed this book, then I'd like to ask you for a favor, would you be kind enough to leave a review for this book on Amazon? It'd be greatly appreciated!

Help us better serve you by sending questions or comments to **greatreadspublishing@gmail.com** - Thank you!

CPSIA information can be obtained
at www.ICGtesting.com
Printed in the USA
FFOW02n1336170117
31457FF